BRAZILIAN JIU-J

Gracie Submission

ESSENTIALS

GRANDMASTER AND MASTER
Secrets of Finishing a Fight

Helio Gracie & Royler Gracie

With Kid Peligro

Photographs by Ricardo Azoury

INVISIBLE CITIES PRESS — MONTPELIER, VERMONT

Invisible Cities Press
41 Northfield Street
Montpelier, VT 05602
www.invisiblecitiespress.com

Library of Congress Cataloging-in-Publication Data
available from the Library of Congress.

ISBN-13: 978-1-931229-45-6
ISBN-10: 1-931229-45-7

Anyone practicing the techniques in this book does so at his or her own risk. The authors and the publisher assume no responsibility for the use or misuse of information contained in this book or for any injuries that may occur as a result of practicing the techniques contained herein. The illustrations and text are for informational purposes only. It is imperative to practice these holds and techniques under the strict supervision of a qualified instructor. Additionally, one should consult a physician before embarking on any demanding physical activity.

Printed in the United States

Book design by Peter Holm, Sterling Hill Productions
Edited by Tia McCarthy and Carmine Grimaldi, Invisible Cities Press

Dedication

Helio Gracie

I carry the dignity of the sport as my flag. I watch over my family name with affection, nerves, and blood.

Royler Gracie

My father once told me that the Jiu-Jitsu that he learned is best described in three words: Blood, sweat and tears. Blood because he had to prove to the world, by fighting bare knuckle no holds barred fights, that Jiu-Jitsu is an efficient fighting style. Sweat, because he worked so hard at it. He sweat many gi's with his efforts to teach hundreds and hundreds of students his art and the efficacy of not only the details but the technique as well. And tears because he gave up doing many things that he liked in order to be the athlete that he always was. He is a person dedicated to the sport like I have never seen in my life.

My first dedication and thanks go to this man without whom many people these days would not be able to eat breakfast, lunch and dinner and carry a lifestyle that is provided to them because of Jiu-Jitsu. Grandmaster Helio today is an icon to anyone that trains or practices martial arts.

Next I have to thank my entire family, my brothers, my cousins and my sisters. Every one of them is involved either directly or indirectly with Jiu-Jitsu. If it weren't for our large family and their involvement and efforts, Jiu-Jitsu would not be what it is today in the spectrum of the martial arts in the world.

I thank the great visionary Sheik Tahnoon bin Zayed Al Nahyan, the man whose idea was to create the first book that I did with my cousin Renzo, *Brazilian Jiu-Jitsu Theory and Technique*. Because of his vision and dream I am now able to continue with an idea and a work that was actually his.

I want to thank my wife and my family for putting up with me. My wife of twenty years has been with me through thick and thin and she is actually my escape valve. My daughters as well. I have four daughters, a 19, 17, 16 and an 8 year old and I can tell you that it is not easy being the wife or daughters of a fighter. When we train hard we bring a lot of energy and problems home and they are the ones that have been my release valve. I know that the person who suffered the most over these years is my wife. I am very happy that we are still together and still love each other and because of her support I am able to accomplish what I have accomplished.

I have to thank my close friend of many years Kid Peligro, who has always helped and supported me in all my projects. He has always been 100% with me, always helping me to do my best.

I have to thank David Adiv and Wellington "Megaton" Dias for their support and friendship over the years. Their total dedication to Jiu-Jitsu has been invaluable.

I have to thank all my friends and supporters and practitioners of Jiu-Jitsu because their words, energy and support are invaluable.

Contents

Royler's favorite submissions

Stand up

Guard Pass

Side Control

Introduction

*T*here are many ways to win a fight or a sports Jiu-Jitsu match; you can win by points, by advantage, by disqualification, but none are as satisfying, as complete and as final as winning by submission. Submission is the KO of Gracie Jiu-Jitsu, the unequivocal way of ending of a fight and the epitome of one's mastery over your opponent. When you submit someone, there is no controversy, there is no doubt, there is only the certainty of the result. You are better than your opponent and he must submit to your technique.

Attack or Wait? Strategies of the Masters

Gracie Jiu-Jitsu is a game of cat and mouse. Both fighters chase each other on the mat trying to get an advantage and better their position until one can finish his opponent with a submission hold. The game at the highest levels is played by two fighters that know enough of the art that there is an ebb and flow of positional gains and losses. As they participate in a match or a sparring session, the real advantage builds from small increments of advances that add up to a solid positional advantage. Sometimes a mistaken decision by one of the participants gives the opportunity of a large advance or a submission to his opponent.

Gracie Jiu-Jitsu is an art of self-defense, in which a smaller, less fit person is given a chance to defend himself and survive an attack by a bigger stronger person. The basis of the art is that the perfect defense not only beats the offense but also allows you to rest, remain calm and conserve energy while forcing your opponent to spend his energy in his attacks until he tires and slows down, allowing the smaller person the opportunities to either escape or even attack and submit his assailant or his opponent.

In Gracie Jiu-Jitsu, as in many martial arts and even real battle, the defense always involves a simpler and more direct path than the attack. The attack generally involves multiple steps while the defense only needs a feint or other simple move. How can you, as an attacker, reach the ability to apply a submission on your opponent? In the next pages Grandmaster Helio and his son Royler Gracie address this problem and give you their individual perspectives on how best to accomplish the task of winning by submission.

Grandmaster Helio Gracie

Grandmaster Helio says, "If you lose it is because you made a mistake, if you don't make any mistakes, you won't lose. I fight not to lose! I never entered a fight thinking about winning. My frame of mind is different – I enter a fight thinking about not losing!"

The Grandmaster believes that when you fight to win you run two risks: you can face a counterattack and be submitted or you can get tired, and when you get tired everything is lost. When you fight to beat someone you add a lot of pressure to yourself and you take risks. When you take chances you give your opponent chances to counterattack. "In my case, fighting not to lose, you play a defensive posture and let your opponent take the chances. He is the one keeping the pressure, he is the one exerting himself, he is the one making mistakes and you are the one ready to capitalize on any mistakes that he makes and perhaps finish the fight there. I take advantage of their mistakes, of their anxiety to end the fight."

Helio Gracie. Personal archives photo.

There is a saying that goes: "If you don't lose, you win!" When you use that philosophy you relax more in a fight and see things that otherwise may go unnoticed when you pressure yourself to finish and win. If you enter the fight not to lose you double your chances of success because you fight with only half of the risk. The attacker always takes the chance of being countered. Grandmaster Helio says, "This philosophy was built into Gracie Jiu-Jitsu, because it was my nature. I always thought 'Why should I attack?' That is my theory, the basis of my martial art. When you fight not to lose you fight a different way than when you fight to win. When you are defensive you always have the chance to counter but when you are attacking you are exposing yourself to the counters."

Jiu-Jitsu arrived in Brazil through Count Koma in the early 1900's. Grandmaster Helio started practicing at age 16 around 1930. "I wanted to do the same things my brother Carlos did but I wasn't as good an athlete as he was. It was impossible for me to fight the way he did. I had to modify those techniques so I could do them, which meant that now anyone could because I was a very weak and non-athletic person. Instead of jumping from a second story roof I built a ladder and stepped down. The end result was the same but I had to use a different way, the way I envisioned I could due to my own physical limitations. Instinctively and out of necessity, I ended up creating a new art that is now practiced around the world: Gracie Jiu-Jitsu. What Carlos and the rest did and learned was more like Judo, based on technique, power and explosion. That is a fight sport for competition. My Jiu-Jitsu is for real fighting. Street fighting."

Grandmaster Helio did not set out to modify the art to become what it is now. As he became more and more involved in everyday teaching at the academy, he continued to modify the art. Every time he was faced with a new difficulty, he was forced to adapt and improve and this still goes on today.

Because of all the changes that Grandmaster Helio made to Jiu-Jitsu, Gracie Jiu-Jitsu is nowadays considered a "new" form of martial art. The Grandmaster points out, "The difference between the old traditional Jiu-Jitsu from Japan is so great from our kind of Jiu-Jitsu that we are now teaching the sport to the Japanese. The value in the Jiu-Jitsu that I practice is that any child, any woman, any senior and even a crippled person can do it. I am over 90 years old, and still teach and practice."

His son Royce proved to the world, by fighting in the Ultimate Fighting Championships, that Jiu-Jitsu is the most efficient martial art in the world. This evolution created many fans and enemies throughout the world. The Gracie family opened the eyes of many to a new way of fighting and the established masters of other styles of martial arts felt threatened.

Royler Gracie

Although he subscribes to his father's philosophy, Royler grew up in a different time. "Growing up at the academy I learned a lot from everyone, but my main influences were my father, and my brothers Rolls and Rickson. They each had their own style, but I liked Rolls's game a lot so I molded my style after his. He had a very aggressive attacking style with a lot of movement and I liked that. He liked to play the top game. His body type was similar to mine. Rolls was the biggest influence in my style of Jiu-Jitsu, bigger than even Rickson. Rickson and my father are my idols, but Rolls was the person whose style I admired and tried to emulate."

Nowadays matches and fights have time restrictions, so Royler had to adapt his game for that: "My father believes in waiting for his opponent's mistakes and attacking when he errs. He doesn't prepare an ambush; he waits for an opportunity. Since the majority of my career matches and fights involved time limits I had to adapt and adjust in order to succeed. I am more aggressive than he is, it is my nature; I like to prepare an ambush. I like to squeeze the opponent and see what he gives me. But this needs to work as a blend of technical knowledge coupled with several combinations and variations of the combinations of the attack that force my opponent to panic and give me what I want."

Royler grew up watching Rorion, Relson, Rickson and Rolls. "Next," he says, "it was my time, and now it is our kids that are fighting. It is a tradition, passed on from generation to generation. Nowadays I go to tournaments and I watch my nephew Kron (Rickson's son) fighting. It is the next chapter of the same story."

Royler continues, "My father likes to say that to be very successful in defense you need to defend the *preparation* of the attack. If you wait to defend the attack you are already late. The defense is always a shorter and faster movement so it is more efficient. The timing of the defense is always shorter than that of the attack. When attacking you always have to prepare, you always have to set up the attack, so the timing is longer, the movement is more complex. So in order to finish someone you need to feign your opponent, you need to be faster than your opponent, you need to be more technical than him. You need to have everything together in order to break him down. The fact that the defense is more efficient forces the attacker to be better at every aspect in order to succeed."

Combinations and sequences of attacks are the best way to achieve the goal of submitting your opponent. Grandmaster Helio believes in a good defense and so does Royler. Both believe that if you want to submit someone, you have to have a strong defense. Then you can be confident that your opponent won't beat you and you can relax and concentrate on seeing his mistakes. Royler says, "I like to prepare an ambush. I like to squeeze the opponent and see what he gives me. But this needs to work in a combinations of technical knowledge coupled with several combinations and variations of the combinations of the attack that force my opponent to panic and give me what I want." (figures 1-4)

In general when Royler decides on a sequence of attacks he knows what the opponent's options are and can anticipate his reactions and counters. He tries to predict the most common escape options and then create a sequence of three to four linked moves based on the expectations of the counters. As he fights, he uses different single attacks to pick up on what his opponent's defense preferences are. Since there's more than one way to counter an attack, he probes his opponent's game to see what his escape preferences are — which ones he does best and which ones he is not so comfortable with. Says Royler, "Once I have that information, I try to guide my attacks and my game to go to the positions where his escapes are weakest and force him to use the ones that he doesn't like. I determine what escapes the opponent likes so I can select a variation of the attack combination that leads to his weakest escapes and also leads to my strongest attacks. For example, if I am mounted on you and you try to use the elbow escape first or more often than the upa, I know that is your preference, so the next time I mount on you, I am going

FIGURE 1

FIGURE 2

FIGURE 3

FIGURE 4

to concentrate on defending the elbow escape and forcing you to use the upa and take advantage of your weakness there. Or I may take the other option. Knowing that you like to use the elbow escape, I will select a good attack that takes advantage of your escape choice such as a "sleeve" choke." With the knowledge of an opponent's preferences, Royler finds he can corner him into a dead end where he has to give him something he already knows is coming, a devastating advantage that will lead to a submission and victory.

The Game

As Royler likes to say, "The game is anticipation." But anticipation does you little good without a solid defense. Since the opponent is countering your every move with moves of his own and wants to achieve the same objective as you, it stands to reason that if you don't have a good defense, you will succumb quicker than he will. The first step to become a good finisher is to develop your defensive skills to the highest level so that you can, even under great pressure from your opponent, relax, maintain your poise and focus on the possibilities of counter-attacks. If during the match you are insecure about your defense, you will be too busy worrying about being submitted to even begin to think about attacking.

With your defense set, the next part of the game is to develop your skills so you can, by virtue of your actions being faster, sharper and more precise than your opponent's, either cut small increments of time until you get an advantage and can apply a move ahead of his defense or induce your opponent to commit a mistake and capitalize on it with a submission.

What it takes to become a good finisher

You have to have great technique, you have to know how to execute the techniques perfectly but once that is achieved you have to have the ability to analyze and react to a situation. Gracie Jiu-Jitsu is a game much like chess: with quick thinking you can plan ahead several moves, giving you a distinct advantage against your opponent. It won't matter if you are very good at individual moves if you don't have a clear plan about what you want to do and where you want to go. The speed of reaction is key then. That doesn't mean you have to be fast or quick, although of course that always helps, but even a slow person with a quick mind can devise and develop a lot of little shortcuts and feints to lead his opponent into a trap. You need to be able to react at the right time.

Throughout your growth in the grappling arts and especially in Gracie Jiu-Jitsu you are introduced to a series of techniques, some of them are directed to gradual advance of your position (escapes and passing the guard, figure 5) some to a sudden advance (sweep or takedowns, figure 6) and some of them are directed towards finishing your opponent via a submission (figure 7). Of all the techniques that you learn, none have more magic or more mystique than the finishing holds, as they give you the power to end a fight with your opponent conceding defeat without appeal as he decides to quit because he faces superior technical knowledge.

FIGURE 5

FIGURE 6

How do you get to apply a submission hold?

While knowledge of individual submission techniques gives you the tools to finish a fight, they are only single pieces of a bigger puzzle. Single techniques are like snap shots; they are a moment frozen in time and only a piece of the ongoing action of a fight. Single techniques are not isolated events; rather, they occur as a result of an action from your opponent during the course of a fight. As you try to apply a submission hold against an opponent you quickly learn that he will fight to defend and escape in addition to responding with attacks of his own. So while it is important to know how to properly execute individual submission holds, it is even more important to learn how to achieve the final objective of applying them against an unwilling opponent. You need to learn how to manipulate the situation so you can successfully apply your technique. You need to know how to think and plan your strategy so you can coax your opponent into giving you the opportunity to use a submission hold. You must learn how to force them into a corner, how to outfox them so they break down and yield to you.

In this book we will convey to you a variety of elements that will turbo-charge your efficiency in becoming a submission expert. In the following pages we will teach you how to think, how to set up and how to best select the techniques to finish your opponent. We will also show you various techniques emphasizing the importance of linking several techniques together so as to confuse and corner your opponent until he falls in the trap and has to tap (submit) admitting defeat.

FIGURE 7

While we cover a lot of ground and try to give you a broad spectrum of thinking, strategy and technical knowledge, we have to remind you that learning Gracie Jiu-Jitsu is not a matter of following a simple set of directions. You must learn to adapt to an ever-changing sequence of movements. Study these pages and expand your thoughts with the newfound knowledge to create your own path and your own "game" so you can become an ever-progressing fighter.

Select techniques to finish your opponent

While there are literally hundreds of finishing holds and variations, knowledge of them all is not necessary, and can even to a certain degree be counter-productive. Since timing and decision-making are a big part of fighting, many times having too many options will slow down the process of selecting the proper technique from all the weapons that you know and want to use. Think about it: if you have only one technique in your arsenal, you will always be quick to select it and use it when the proper situation occurs, as it is your only choice. However, if you have 100 options, when an opportunity occurs you now have to consider all those choices before deciding which one is best to use. That of course does not mean you shouldn't learn several techniques, but keep in mind, especially in the beginning of your training, less can mean more. Having a few great weapons may give you an edge over someone who has many mediocre weapons and is slower at selecting and applying them.

While all techniques should work for everyone, realistically, because of your build, nature and physical characteristics, some techniques will work better for you than others. For instance, if you have long legs your triangle will be better than if you have short legs. Of course not many people know which techniques will be most effective for them before they start, so learn the techniques, practice them and try to apply them. As you train more and more, you will notice that you favor certain submission techniques more than others and those are the ones you should, at least at first, concentrate on and develop. Grandmaster Helio likes to say: "The sport adapts itself to each body type and each individual's strengths and weaknesses. It actually molds itself to the characteristics of each individual."

It is quite common and healthy for you, at least in the beginning, to have one submission that is considered to be "yours". Some like to base their game on the choke, while others like to base it on another submission like the arm-lock. Once you have selected your favorite submission, you should further develop it and learn how to apply it from a variety of situations. Once you are very good at using that submission, you will force your opponents to defend it and even fear it, to the point where they will give you open-

"Before I fought I had an open mind. I had no fear." Helio focused before a match. Personal archives photo.

ings for other attacks. At that point go to the second strongest submission in your arsenal and try to incorporate it with your main submission, giving you a second option and creating more confusion for your opponents.

When you do this in a match or while sparring, try to keep mental notes of which move works best for you and when. If the choke works often, try improving on it and increase the frequency of using it. Watch what caused the opening for your attack to occur: did you feign a move to set up that choke, or did you wait for your opponent to commit to something? By noting when the technique worked best and why, and which combinations are most effective for you, you'll develop a mental trigger for it and for other sequences of attacks.

Royler's game, like his father's, is based on the choke. The choke opens up a lot of possibilities and creates a lot of difficulties. The choke leads to many other submissions. Once you establish that you are good at one submission like the choke, your opponents will pay an inordinate amount of attention to your preparation of the choke and will many times over-react to it, leading to many openings for other moves. You may find you like arm-locks and foot-locks as well, however the choke fits nicely into the mix. Royler says, "I told my dad once: 'Dad I really like arm-locks'. He came back and said: 'I like chokes better.' To which I replied yes but you have two arms to attack and only one neck. And he retorted: 'Yes but the arm you have to break and the opponent may still continue to fight. The choke, once applied he either submits or he is out!' I learned a lot from that conversation and changed my game because of that."

As you get better at synchronizing your attacks with two options, use the same criteria to add another technique, whether a finishing hold or a sweep, to open up the game even more and give you more options and create even more difficulties for your adversary.

Power, Timing, and Execution

Royler believes that three factors are most important in succeeding as a fighter and as a finisher: they are power, speed of thought (timing) and technique execution.

Objective Strength and Power

After you properly repeat a position several times in your practice and your training you will notice and your training partners will also notice that you develop a certain strength that is called "objective strength". Objective strength is when all the elements of the mechanics of the position coupled with your development of the specific muscles involved in that particular position are aligned and working together in unison with the objective of applying the greatest amount of power capable without over-exerting or tightening the muscles. To develop this type of power you need practice and repetition of the technique with perfect form.

The Mantra of Submissions: Timing and Execution

The key to becoming a good Gracie Jiu-Jitsu fighter is best summarized in two words: Timing and Execution. As you begin your path in Gracie Jiu-Jitsu and start testing your skills against equal level opponents, initially you may be able to succeed without having all the elements in place. White and blue belts sometimes can finish their opponents relying on single attacks. However as your skill level improves and you start taking on better and more skilled opponents you will find that to catch someone in a submission hold, you have to weave a path that involves many elements, such as feints, traps and techniques linked together.

At the higher levels, it is much harder to induce your opponent to make a mistake you can use to catch him. The keys to success at those levels are timing and execution. To catch the best you need to be able to execute the perfect technique at the right time.

Timing

Everything in life is about timing. Buy the ticket with the six winning Lotto numbers on the wrong day and you end up with nothing but a piece of paper instead of becoming an instant millionaire. Jiu-Jitsu is much like life, if your timing is wrong even the best and most perfectly executed technique will fail. You may anticipate your opponent's moves and even recognize the opening for an arm-lock, but you select the wrong technique or you are slow to react in applying the attack and your timing is off. For example, if you apply the arm-lock when your opponent has already pulled his arm out, your attack only helps him pass your guard. In Gracie Jiu-Jitsu timing is applying a combination of four major elements — Anticipation, Recognition, Selection, and Reaction — at the correct moment. When you have all four elements working well together, your timing is perfect. You are always slightly ahead of your opponent and leading him down the path to submission. Let's examine these elements and see how you can improve them.

Anticipation

Anticipation is one of the keys to success in your quest to become a good finisher. Anticipation is the ability to see what is coming and even think and plan a few moves ahead. When you are sparring or fighting, the ability to foresee your opponent's next move allows you to cuts precious milliseconds of time. Since the defense has a timing advantage, any time you are able to find the slightest shortcut you will gain a great edge. Anticipation develops from being on the mat training and observing others training around you. In Gracie Jiu-Jitsu there are always certain sequences of moves that are connected together and there are certain patterns of reactions that can be detected. For example, when you mount someone, he will generally try to escape with an "upa" or an elbow escape (figures 8-10) depending on his preference and the kind of attack or posture you take. By knowing either his normal reaction or the typical escape route, you can anticipate what the opponent will do and get ready to advance to the next step, thus getting ahead of him in the sequence.

FIGURE 8

FIGURE 9

FIGURE 10

Now when you examine this further by either sparring or watching others spar, you will start to see that certain patterns occur more frequently than others. By noticing such patterns and practicing them, your brain and neuro-motor skills will be faster and eventually automatic when one of those sequences arise. Once you have developed the mental picture and understanding of one of these sequences, however short they may be, start training with a willing partner and experimenting with the options that occur.

The next step in developing this skill, of course, is applying it on the mat against an unwilling partner. See what works and what problems and unpredictable situations arise and try to solve them. The final step in this development is to spar with a person and get to the point when you can submit them and allow them (without telling them) to escape the attack. At that point you will be developing not only anticipation but recognition.

Recognition

Although it seems similar to its previous partner, recognition is different from anticipation. Recognition is the ability to understand a certain move or attack as it is happening whether it was anticipated or not. Recognition involves being able to discern by the slightest of hints, such as a certain grip or a hip position or any other signal, whether the opponent is attacking your arm or your neck or setting you up for a sweep or another such move.

Developing your recognition involves many of the same exercises as developing anticipation. Sparring, paying attention to others sparring, and being very sensitive to what your opponent is doing all help in developing this skill. One of the keys to developing your recognitive skills is being able to train relaxed. If you train tense or use a lot of power and hold your opponent, you will hinder your ability to sense his moves, especially the subtle ones such as a slight weight shift or a tension of his arm that may precede an attack or an attempted sweep. When you are relaxed you are able to sense your opponent's body moves and language and are able to better "read" his intentions.

Reaction

You may be able to anticipate your opponent's moves and recognize them clearly and early but you may not react to them quickly enough, losing most of the edge that you've gained. Being able to connect your body and mind so that the moment you recognize what is coming or what is available you instantly react to it, will greatly increase your success at submitting your opponents.

In Gracie Jiu-Jitsu, "reaction" is your ability to move or adjust your body a certain way as a result of a situation. Reaction is naturally built into every animal, including of course human beings. When someone throws something at your face, you instinctively close your eyes and place your hands in front of the face to protect it. That same instantaneous and almost spontaneous reaction can and should be developed for Jiu-Jitsu.

Selection

While you may have all of the previous elements of success for a submission, your ability to quickly and properly select the right technique for the moment is of paramount importance. All that anticipation, recognition and reaction do for you is put you at the right place at the right time. The next big key is to be able to select the best technique for *you* to apply at that exact moment. Selection is a key that can be developed and perfected much like the others. Simple methods of improving selection are explained earlier in this book, however one can also learn and improve his selection ability by observing his and others' results in training and fighting.

FIGURE 10

For maximum efficiency and best results it is important that you select the best technique that you are *capable of executing* at any time, even if that is not the best technique option. When you select the best technique for a situation but you are not capable of properly executing it, your technical mistake will cause everything else to crumble. For example, you are in side control and trap your opponent's arm. At that point you can apply an arm-lock (figure 10), a kimura (figure 11) or a key-lock (figure 12). Of the three options the kimura is your weakest and the key-lock your strongest, so the smart choice for you would be to go for the key-lock to increase your chances of success.

Of course as you progress in the art and get more advanced and fight against more advanced fighters, you will need to improve and increase your arsenal of techniques to the point where you have at least two to three good technical options for any situation.

FIGURE 11

Execution

At this point you have mastered the four elements of timing (Anticipation, Recognition, Selection, Reaction) and in grand form you apply the perfect technique choice at the exact moment and expect the best result: your opponent tapping in admission of your technical superiority! Instead however, your opponent escapes, leaving you with nothing but frustration and perhaps in a worse position than you started with. What has failed? Your technical form is weak, giving your

FIGURE 12

opponent plenty of options to foil your attack. This is where we go back to the basics. As in the end of a match, when you have finally cornered your opponent and reached the point of applying the submission hold, you are back to the ability to precisely execute a single, basic technique in order to succeed.

Practice and repetition of every basic and advanced single submission technique with a willing partner is the perfect way to improve and master them. Start off by repeating a single technique numerous times against a willing partner. For instance do ten arm-locks from the guard to each arm before each training session. Concentrate on perfect form as with each repetition you are training your body and mind to execute a move perfectly. If you try to speed up and do the repetitions quickly at first, you may not do the technique perfectly, and you would be teaching your body and mind to be good at doing something wrong! After you feel comfortable with the initial number of repetitions and your technical mastery of them, increase the number of repetitions. Eventually you should start to increase the speed of applying the technique but *never* at the cost of form. Remember, Grandmaster Helio and Master Royler both emphasize technical perfection, and good speed is a consequence of repetition in perfect form.

As you master speed and technique against a willing partner, have him increase the difficulty in his defense in small increments until you are able to execute the move against him even when he is resisting. At that point you have mastered that submission technique and can go on to trying to use it in sparring.

How you develop these traits

You first start using a simple combination of two attacks that work together. Once you have mastered the counter options and the normal reactions to that simple attack you can go ahead and add another. It is very important to spend time on the mat practicing first the individual techniques and attacks. If you cannot properly execute an arm-lock, there is no point trying to combine it with another move. First you need to master a few moves perfectly. Repetition is one key to mastering a move. You must use it over and over against a series of different opponents, people of different sizes, weights and reactions. First start with a willing partner and repeat the move until it becomes automatic. At that point have your partner give you a harder time and slowly increase the difficulty level of his defense.

Once you are comfortable using it against your partner it is time to try the move in sparring. When you are trying a new move you should always begin with the lightest and least experienced fighter you can find. That is because it is hard enough to use a move against another fighter who has a mind of his own and wants to defend your attacks. You need to be able to control the training and direct your partner to a position where you can repeat the attack over and over until you can quickly and easily execute it against him at will. If you attempt to use a new move, one that you have not yet fully mastered, against a more advanced or stronger opponent, your chances of failure are greatly increased. You may not be able to repeat the position again because you are not able to control or direct the sparring session. You may then become frustrated and decide that the technique doesn't work and give up on it altogether.

Once you are comfortable with the technique against the lightest, least skilled fighter your next step is to use a heavier opponent with a low skill level. You should increase the weight first and then after you have mastered the use of the technique against the heaviest fighter of that level you can go up in skill, once again start at the bottom of the weight scale and go up until you have the heaviest. Proceed in this manner until you are capable of using the technique against the heaviest and most skilled fighters in your academy.

It is very important to be proficient at executing each of the basic submissions before you try to combine them. If you can't execute one technique then linking two together will only create havoc for yourself. Once you have mastered a single technique try using the same training method now and combine two techniques together. Go through the same process and after you have mastered a two-attack combination then proceed to add another option.

If you introduce another option to the choke - in this case, the arm-lock - your opponent will have to divide his attention between two moves giving you twice the opportunity to achieve your goal. Since you have the lead in deciding which and when to change, you are able to shorten the timing advantage that the defense has.

How you develop quickness

First you need to train without worrying. You shouldn't worry about competition; you shouldn't worry about becoming a fighter or even becoming good at Jiu-Jitsu. That is different from the reality of many people who start training nowadays. They come in and sign up already thinking or dreaming or planning on becoming a top fighter. That kind of pressure creates a barrier and a difficulty that is not conducive to becoming a great finisher. Because the objectives are somewhat immediate, they develop a game for tournaments, and a game to win by the rules. They are not worried about creating a game that encourages submissions, because the win for them is the same and it is easier to win by points or advantages than by submission. So they focus on narrow paths and on immediate results rather than the longer path that it takes to become a good finisher. To become a good finisher you need to try to attack and apply submissions. Your rate of failure increases (as we have seen the Grandmaster tell) when you press the issue and try the ultimate tools of concluding a fight. It is much safer for instance to remain in side-control and wait for time to end a match than it is to try to mount or go for an arm-lock from the side. When you try to mount or go for the arm-lock you are giving your opponent a chance to escape and even advance his position in relation to yours. The person with an immediate objective and the pressure of winning always and early on will not take that chance and therefore will not develop his submission skills.

It is through failure and repetition that you sharpen your attacks and your submissions. If you don't attempt them you won't perfect them. Train relaxed and try to use your submissions. Pressure creates a barrier against advancing. You need to have a clear and open mind to learn and progress. Let the game flow without pressing. When you try to force attacks the opponent closes up and it becomes even harder to submit him.

A good way to develop your submissions is to train with someone less skilled than you. If you catch him on something, let go of the submission before he taps, let him escape and go for the next submission and so forth. This approach will allow you to accomplish a number of objectives. First, your partner will like training with you a lot more because he is not just tapping and being submitted left and right. He will be less inclined to tighten up in order to avoid being submitted constantly. Second, you will go through many more positions and submission attempts than if you continually catch him and force the sparring session to start over. Third, by letting him escape, you will learn the most natural escape patterns and learn to anticipate and adjust to the escapes and apply your next technique sharpening the "mantra of the submissions": timing and execution.

Relaxing affects your opponent's mindset. When you corner a mouse against the wall, no matter how small he is he will feel threatened and attack you. However if you pretend you don't see him, he will relax and you can go and catch him! The same approach works for humans: when you apply incessant pressure your opponent will close up with all his might. Since the defense is more efficient it will become harder for you to catch him. If you relax and let the game flow without showing your real intentions your opponent will relax more and take more chances, allowing you more opportunities to catch him. That is the key: let your opponent feel so relaxed and without a worry that he exposes himself more.

Of course putting pressure on someone can also induce him to make mistakes, but there is a limit to the level of pressure, otherwise he falls into the overly defensive mentality. If you want to evolve technically you need to train relaxed without the pressures of progressing or of having to produce immediate results. One of Royler's favorite ways to surprise someone is to attack and persist for a little while and then let go as if giving up. When the opponent feels the threat abate, he'll relax also and Royler comes back with the same attack to submit him. Try it yourself. Attack your partner's arm with an arm-lock (figure 13). At first he will defend with all his might and hold onto his arm and put his weight on your legs to crush you. If you relax and appear to let go, he is likely to relax as well. Then you can go back and pry his arm free and extend your legs to complete the submission.

Learning never stops in Gracie Jiu-Jitsu. The Master and Grandmaster both are to this date learning new things and even more details about the basic things. As Royler says, "I always went to the academy without any worries about winning or submitting anyone. I have always been a very friendly person and I'd go to the academy to enjoy the moment and the people there and of course to train. I always loved being in the academy, I felt that made me have a forward, open game."

The new kids and new students starting today should have that in mind. Try to think of being like a child having fun training. A kid has no pressure – he just wants to have fun. With that attitude you keep an open mind and learn quickly. One of

FIGURE 13

Royler's techniques to get his students to relax is to talk to them and make fun of things in training even when they are sparring. A few of them take things too seriously, and even in a private lesson train as if their lives depended on the result of that session. Talking and having fun breaks that frame of mind, and shows them that Jiu-Jitsu is fun.

Training Partners

Partner selection is a very important aspect of becoming proficient at Gracie Jiu-Jitsu and especially so at becoming a good finisher. Royler likes to train with people of his weight. He believes that he improves more when he trains with people of similar size and weight. Avoid those opponents that use abnormal amounts of power when training. If you are constantly battling with power you can get injured and your training doesn't develop because you are not relaxed. The person who is tense and uses a lot of power slows himself and his partners. Try training with the partners who train in control and are not reckless and who are as intent in progressing as you are. Of course there are different training requirements. If you are going to compete or if you are going to be in an NHB fight, then the partners and the objectives are different than for the normal person and even for the competitor. The proper selection of the sparring or training partners is key to achieving your goal.

When you train with someone, you can capture their energy. You can tell when they are out to hurt you, when they are nice and train light. You can tell when the person is rough and uses a lot of power. When you are teaching you get in tune with those things and you can tell what the student is doing and how he is reacting to your teaching. This is a very important aspect to develop because this connection also lets you understand when the person gives up or is getting frustrated with your attacks or with your pressure and is ready to be taken and be submitted. Being connected emotionally to the opponent lets you sense when he is feeling pressured and exasperated. Sometimes you are attacking and are not sure of your success but if you are connected you can sense his level of intensity rise or his desperation or frustration increase as you move forward and that gives you an edge to pursue the course further rather than give up and start over from a different position or attack. This connection also allows you to sense when he is distracted or when he is getting tired. When he is distracted you have the opportunity to go for a submission. When you sense he is getting tired you can increase the pace or the pressure more to sap whatever energy he has left and have him "die out" on you and be ready to be taken out.

Training Gracie Jiu-Jitsu is a form of therapy. When you are there you forget everything; you forget all your problems. You forget about the bills you have to pay, the fight with the neighbor, the problems at work, everything. Of course when you finish it all comes back, but because Jiu-Jitsu is a fighting martial art it also teaches you to deal with a lot of real life situations not related to fighting. When you train you are put into difficult situations, pressure situations that you can escape only by staying relaxed and being able to think clearly. With your training you learn how to stay calm in real life situations.

Royler has been teaching since he was 14 years old, but he became an instructor when he was 16. He was a blue-purple belt and would assist Rickson in his classes and cover for him when couldn't show up to teach. He has been teaching for 23 years. Royler says "I learned a lot from teaching. Teaching forces you to look and learn the details of each technique. You have to go to the depths of understanding the technique in order to be able to fully convey it to someone else. Because when you teach you have to not only be able to explain the technique so the student understands it, but you also have to see the technique from his side, see the difficulties that he is having to learn and replicate the move and then find a way to correct or adjust or modify the technique so he can learn it and use it. You have to be like a mirror and visualize everything from both sides and understand everything from your and your student's perspective. You have to see the difficulties and the solutions of every problem."

Royler always has a smile on his face when he is teaching. "I love teaching and I've never been forced to do it. If I didn't feel like teaching there wouldn't be enough money in the world to get me on the mat. But the truth is that I enjoy teaching and I enjoy conveying techniques to another person and watching the person grow as a student. I enjoy the relationships that I have developed over the years because of teaching and because of Jiu-Jitsu. Everyday when I go to the school to teach I have a smile on my face and I do it with pleasure. If I don't like the person I won't teach him either. It is my job of course but it is also a pleasure. Not a day goes by when I get up and don't feel like teaching. I may wake up tired but I am always looking forward to teaching."

A conversation with the Grandmaster

How did you get involved in Jiu-Jitsu?
When I was young I was very frail and suffered from fainting spells. It became such a problem that after a few years I stopped going to school, staying home instead. I would watch my older brother Carlos teach Jiu-Jitsu. One day when I was young Carlos was late for a private lesson and the student asked me if I wanted to 'play' until Carlos got there. I ended up teaching him the class. When Carlos arrived, excusing himself for being late, the student excitedly dismissed the issue and told Carlos that he wanted me to be his instructor from then on. That was the day that I became an instructor. And that created another problem—now I had to do the things that I had learned by watching.

What factors influenced your approach to Jiu-Jitsu?
Jiu-Jitsu appeared in my life because my brother Carlos learned it from a Japanese man (Count Koma). The count taught him the Jiu-Jitsu that they practiced in Japan, the Jiu-Jitsu that we practice today and is practiced around the world, I practically created it. That is the Jiu-Jitsu adapted to my person, the Jiu-Jitsu practiced around the world today is a refined Jiu-Jitsu full of finesse. The basic principles are leverage and technique.

Bigger, stronger Carlos was a much better athlete, and he had built an aggressive style of Jiu-Jitsu around one's ability to overpower an opponent. But that wouldn't work for me. I couldn't do most of the moves, but I strived hard to find ways to adapt them to my abilities. All my life I have been very determined, and I took it as a challenge to find ways to do the moves. So I began experimenting with different leverages and adjustments. I often say that a child is great, because a child is always improvising to get around in a world designed for adults. So I started to study the leverage points on the human body. If you use leverage, you can multiply your effect many times over, much like you use a jack to lift a car. You can't lift a car, but when you use a jack you can easily lift it. I simply adapted the use of a "jack" to every position of Jiu-Jitsu. And that became the sport we have today. I made the sport accessible to the weakling so he could defend against a strong person—and now even the strong ones must learn my techniques so they don't get spanked by a weakling!

What was teaching like for you? What did Carlos think of your approach?
When I took over the duties at the Gracie Academy I was teaching forty classes a day, starting at 6:00 A.M. and working until 9:00 P.M. I went through sixteen gis each day! This dedication left Carlos free to concentrate on managing the academy. Because we were both so busy in our duties, for a while we never exchanged information about what was going on. I had no time to sit down with him and show him all the changes I had made. For his part, since the students were all happy, he saw no reason to quiz me about the day-to-day lessons. One day, I felt that I had developed the sport in so many ways that I had better let Carlos know what was happening. I went up to the office to talk to him. Carlos listened, but instead of

acknowledging *my* achievements, he singled out another instructor, praising his strength and skills, indicating that I was not in that league. I replied that he was wrong, that I could beat that guy and the three other instructors in twenty minutes. Carlos laughed and said, "If I match him with you, he is going to turn you inside out." So we made a bet to see if I could do it. Carlos scheduled the challenge for the next day.

The next day we met at the academy. Carlos told me that I didn't have to go through with it, but I knew this was my chance to show my brother how effective my innovations were. I finished the first three instructors in seven minutes, one after the other. Then I turned to Carlos and said, "Do you think it will take me thirteen minutes to finish the last one?" I defeated the fourth instructor in five minutes. Carlos was astounded.

Inseparable! Helio throws Carlos.
Personal archives photo.

Every fight I did was a testing ground for the efficiency of the techniques that I did, I kept testing and improving the techniques as the necessities of real fights and real life demanded.

Grandmaster fought many fights in his career including fights against Japanese Champions Kato and Kimura and his last major fight was the longest fight in the history of modern fighting: a 3 hour and 45 minute bout against his former student Waldemar Santana. Grandmaster also used his students as testing grounds, making sure to perfect his techniques as the students showed him difficulties in using them.

I never taught anyone how to compete. I always taught people how to fight! I was never a competitor; I was and always will be a fighter. My Jiu-Jitsu was created as a means of self-defense, so the weak can beat the strong; nowadays a lot of strong people are learning it because they don't want to be beaten by a weaker person with knowledge of Jiu-Jitsu. But the strong ones have a harder time learning the details and nuances because they tend to use their strength to compensate any technical flaws, they don't have to learn it perfect even though they can, because their strength makes up for their flaws. But if you take a strong person and teach them Jiu-Jitsu, even when they are not perfect they greatly improve as fighters. But the weaker person has to do it perfectly otherwise he is in trouble so the weak person generally always looks for the details and how to execute it perfectly. That is why children learn it perfectly: they learn how to do the movement the perfect way and as they grow bigger and stronger they add the strength to the technical perfection, making them very efficient.

Please tell us more about your approach to Jiu-Jitsu.

We had hundreds of students. At one time we had 600 students and were teaching 600 classes a week. In my view a technique is only a good technique if it works for everyone. If you show me a technique that only works for people who are strong or flexible or fast or whatever; then in my view it is not a good technique. For me to consider a technique to be a good one it *has* to work for everyone; a small weak person has to be able to successfully execute it. My techniques work for anyone; even if you are weak you can apply them, so long as you learn them correctly. I developed a system of leverages that work for anyone. The Jiu-Jitsu I created is based on leverage; no one can take my arm if I have the proper leverage. The positions are all based on points of leverage, the power of leverage is different than muscle power. If I place my arm a certain way you can sit on it and I won't even feel it; if I place it a different way I may not be able to sustain ten pounds! The difference is almost invisible to the regular person, even a good fighter. Only a person that has been exposed to the right technical knowledge can see and appreciate the subtle differences between the right way and the okay way to execute techniques. For instance, if I place my elbow on a surface and hold an object with my hand I can sustain or even lift a lot more weight than if my entire arm is suspended and not touching anything! That is an example of the power of leverage and the leverages that are built into all humans. All that was developed because I was a weakling growing up. I was always a light guy, the heaviest I ever got was 63 kg; so I always had to have the perfect technique for things to work. The entire time I was looking for these leverages and how to apply them and how to transmit that power. Therefore I am always fighting, making effort and trying to use the things that I created in my own self, I am always looking to use and apply the leverages that are built into our own body! Once you know what they are and how to use them then you have the essence of what I teach.

Kimura and Helio locked in battle.
Personal archives photo.

Revista "O Cruzeiro" depicts Helio's feats. Personal archives photo.

Why do you think Gracie Jiu-Jitsu is such an effective art?

Human beings are great at adapting. If you try to go through a door that only a 5-year old child can fit through, you will find that you can't. So you have to either open the door or make the hole bigger or you can't get through. I wasn't able to do the things that my brother Carlos was doing because he was a very fast man. Very fast and athletic and agile and I wasn't as athletic as he was. So the problem became, how do I do the things that he does if I don't have the same physical characteristics. I started to diminish my goals and create better leverage points. So my Jiu-Jitsu does not depend on physical abilities nor physical

strength, it is purely dependent on technique. For you to get an idea any man has more power on his finger than any other man has on his hand! That was the marvel of the leverages that I created in order to be able to make my Jiu-Jitsu. I suffered quite a bit, but little by little I adapted myself to the positions. It wasn't really a matter of intelligence as much as a process of adaptation. I couldn't get through the hole, so I made the hole bigger and then I went through it! I didn't dream at the time that the hole that I had just opened would become the same hole to give everyone a path to get through.

Nature is extremely wise and has given us the elements for us to survive and overcome certain physical shortcomings that we may have. It is up to us to discover and develop and make use of them.

Tell us more about the role of leverage in Gracie Jiu-Jitsu.

There is a big difference between physical power and the power of leverage and technique. In physical power you are always exerting yourself and spending energy. When you use the power of leverage and technique you can relax, therefore you last longer and you can think more clearly.

With the perfect technique you don't need power. For instance, when you want to choke someone you just need to apply pressure to the arteries on the side of the neck. You can do that with just two fingers! So when you apply the choke you need to be able to set your technique so it applies pressure there, there is an adjustment that is almost imperceptible to the normal person but the expert knows what it is and how to do it. My favorite submission is the choke. I fought sixteen fights and won most of them by choke!

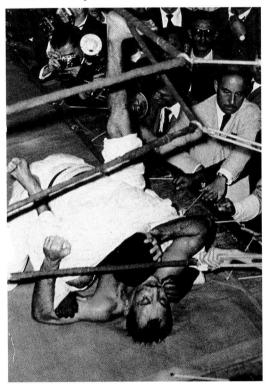

The longest fight in history: Helio v. Waldemar.
Personal archive photo.

What was your most important fight?

My most important fight was against Kimura. Despite the fact that Carlos threw in the towel I still consider it the fight that gave me the most international fame. I used to try to instigate the Japanese to come and fight me. I would say: "They send the Japanese fighters to come to sleep in Brazil?" I wanted to test myself against the best.

To do what I did at the age that I was, the weight and the strength that I had is a miracle! I fought Zbyszko who weighed 265 pounds and I weighed 132, when I was 42 years old I fought Waldemar Santana, who was 23 years younger and 66 pounds heavier, in a single round fight that lasted 3 hours and 45 minutes. I was able to do that because I fight not to lose. I don't get tired because I don't attack. I don't fight to win; I fight not to lose! The attacker always takes the chance of being countered. This philosophy was built into Gracie Jiu-Jitsu, because it was my nature. I always thought why should I attack, that is my theory, the basis of my martial. When you fight not to lose you fight a different way than when you fight to win. When you are defensive you always have the chance to counter but when you are attacking you are exposing yourself to the counters.

Seeing the opportunity to counter is something you develop naturally after many hours of training. It is a natural instinct, when someone punches you to defend yourself. When someone pokes at your eyes you instinctively close them and place a hand in front and duck your head. All that is part of your natural instincts. When someone is punching at your face, you defend and then sometimes you see an opening and you punch back. It is spontaneous, natural reaction to being attacked. So when you train enough, you begin to instinctively see the openings and the opportunities to counter-attack. Of course you have to learn the techniques, be capable of applying them perfectly in a controlled environment and master them before you are capable of using them in practice or sparring against someone else.

You have to keep in mind that at that time most of the fights had no time limits so a big part of my strategy was to defend and tire the bigger, stronger, more athletic opponent. Nowadays with the short rounds you may have to fight different. In a 10-minute fight you have to attack otherwise your may end up with a draw. The shorter the round, the more risks you have to take but my philosophy remains the same and that is the strength of Jiu-Jitsu.

How is Royler's style like yours?

My son Royler is very similar to me, physically and his face looks like mine. He also likes to choke people. I like to say that there are no brave fighters when it comes to a choke. When you catch someone in a joint lock, they may be able to resist because they are strong or even fight after their joint is damaged, but in the case of the choke, they either submit or they go to sleep so it is a very definite way to end a fight. No question about it. Because of that the choke is a great set up for other submissions.

FIGURE 14

Royler is the best in the world at his weight, he learned the technique and with his intelligence he developed his own style and he won everything. He learned the art by being around us, being around Jiu-Jitsu all the time. He would watch us train and teach, when he had a question he would come and ask. He grew up in the academy and around fighters so it was natural that he developed the way he did.

Our guard (figure 14), connecting the leg movement with the choke and the arm-lock is very strong, our Jiu-Jitsu in general is good because it is based on that. If you fall between my legs (guard) it is hard for you to escape without being submitted. Because when you do something I attack your neck. It is hard to pass without exposing your neck and I base my guard defense on attacking the neck (figure 15). That opens up a lot of other options. Since I modified the passing techniques, I know exactly where the weakness is and how to break it down. I know where the hole is so I avoid falling into it. Also I know how to lead my opponent to the hole!

FIGURE 15

Are you still very involved in Jiu-Jitsu?

My concentration in the sport is constant. Ever since that day that I first taught, all my life has been dedicated to this sport, how to improve it as a sport, as a martial art, as a fighting style and as a life style. I spend my entire existence to better Jiu-Jitsu, and that is why I fought so many fights, because I needed to test it and improve upon it. Now I am older and I don't have the same worries in life but I still try to watch what others are doing and try to find their difficulties and their mistakes and look for ways to improve on them.

Yes, I still teach, but I have very few students. I have a few people that still want me to be their teacher because they like my style. One of the things that helped me is that because I was such a weakling physically, I had to compensate that by improving the technique. I value the technique above everything and the student would see that. If I was heavy and strong, the student would be unsure if things were working because I was strong or heavy or if indeed it was because of the technique.

Take Royler for instance, who I consider one of the best instructors amongst my sons, he impresses everyone because he is so light, if you took Carlson or Rickson at 90 kilos (198 lbs) the student is not sure and wonders: 'Is he just strong or this is working because of technique?' With Royler, they don't have any doubts!

The biggest reason I feel very fortunate about being involved in this sport is because of all the participants that we have and all the people that I have met and friends that I have and that I have been able to help them better their lives a little bit!

What was your preparation for a fight?

Before I fought I always had an open mind. I had no fear, because I knew that I wasn't going to lose and that was based on the fact that I wanted not to lose. I wanted to see how he was going to beat me? I test myself and test my techniques.

I believe that preparation and knowledge are the keys to succeeding in any situation. With the right preparation and the proper knowledge you can overcome any hurdle, surpass any obstacle and defeat any opponent. The key is knowledge and preparation! What people call luck I prefer to call merit! You get what you deserve by merit. I always tried to tackle any challenge, I was never afraid of anything, to this day I am not afraid of anything. You can send me to the jungle to face a lion. I will go but I will be prepared to face the lion, with a good rifle I will face any lion. It is when you try to face an attack without having the proper conditions to react that you lose. Whatever challenge you throw my way I will take it, but I will prepare myself to face the conditions of the challenge. It is not crazy courage, it is an understanding of a situation and a preparation to face the demands of the challenge. I am not stupid, I just don't go into any dark hole. Before I go in I want to know how deep, how wide and what is at the bottom of the hole. Once I know that I determine what I'll need and then go in fully. Many people who believe they are brave would just go in and then get destroyed, they want to show courage but they fail to evaluate the challenge and what is at stake! And they fail because they are caught unprepared, it is the counter-attack from nature the same counter-attack that works in a fight! I examine everything with good sense and then I prepare for whatever and whoever I am going to face.

The analysis and preparation to face any challenge, any situation, any enemy and any opponent are some of the most important things one can do. Take the advice and apply to situations such as facing an opponent in a NHB match or in a Gracie Jiu-Jitsu competition. Grandmaster's son Master Royler is a firm believer of that philosophy as he always takes great pride in his preparation both physical and mental before facing any opponent.

Tell us more about your sons and their individual styles.

When I watch a son of mine fighting, I believe they are going to win. If they apply their knowledge and execute the theory that I use they win. Our Jiu-Jitsu is the most perfect martial art there is. There is nothing more efficient than our Jiu-Jitsu. If you deviate from the technique then you lose. If you lose it is because you made a mistake, if you don't make any mistakes, you won't lose. Rickson is the best fighter of the family because he is the stronger, technically they are all equal, if you want a lighter fighter take Royler, he is the best at his weight. Really Royler is very similar to me. *Royler is the image of the Grandmaster, many of his friends call him Helio Gracie Jr not only because of his physical similarity but because Royler has always strived to follow his father's footsteps. He has always looked to do similar challenges like fighting bigger fighters entering many different types of competitions and never backing away from an opponent because of weight and strength differences many times entering the Absolute division in Gracie Jiu-Jitsu competitions facing the biggest fighters and also fighting in MMA against top fighters that outweigh him.*

Like father, like son. Helio and Royler amused during the 2002 Dynamite event in Tokyo, Japan. Photo: Kid Peligro.

I have sons everywhere, in Brazil, in Spain, in the USA. Nowadays they practice Gracie Jiu-Jitsu everywhere in this World. I am the creator of this art, now they practice it even in Japan, where the initial art came from. I am very famous there as well. *In the space of his lifetime Grandmaster has seen the martial art that he developed conquer the world. Gracie Jiu-Jitsu is practiced in the five continents. Grandmaster was the one chosen to light up the Olympic torch at the National Stadium in Tokyo in front of 90,000 fans for Dynamite event in 2001.*

l-r Rolker, Royler, Helio, Royce and Robin, Dynamite event, Tokyo, Japan 2002. Photo: Kid Peligro.

Rorion took Jiu-Jitsu to the USA and because of his sacrifice of leaving Brazil and building a base in the USA and developing the UFC where Royce introduced Jiu-Jitsu to the world. The world now practices Jiu-Jitsu and he was the one that gave the initial push for the expansion of Jiu-Jitsu beyond Brazil throughout the world. Relson went to Hawaii and teaches Jiu-Jitsu there. He introduced the art to the Hawaiian Islands and he is part of the family members that traveled outside Brazil and spread the seeds of Jiu-Jitsu around.

Rickson lives in LA. now and he is considered the best fighter in the world along with Royce. I am very happy to see that the power of Jiu-Jitsu is so strong that they can live wherever they want to live and do the things they do. Rolker for instance has an academy attended by hundreds of students each day in Rio where the competition for students is tough.

Rolker is a great instructor and co-leader of the Gracie Rio de Janeiro academy.

Royler is a great champion with a storied career.

Royce is a formidable fighter that has demonstrated to everyone how great he is. When Royce first fought in the UFC no one knew Jiu-Jitsu, so he defeated all opponents from various martial arts very easily because of his Jiu-Jitsu skills.

Robin is in Europe spreading the gospel of Jiu-Jitsu in Spain.

Do you feel accomplished with the sons that you have?

Royce told something once that I never forget: "My father told me never to be lazy and that is something I've always done in my life. I am always looking to work and to be busy."

You have seven sons and two daughters and we are all busy and good workers do you get a sense of accomplishment from that?

I believe I lead by example. When a son doesn't have a father that shows them the way by doing it then they have nothing to go by. I have always led by example and then my sons and daughters all followed in my footsteps but in their own way. All my kids are brave, honest and are a great source of pride to me.

Can you tell us about some effective techniques in Gracie Jiu-Jitsu?

When someone is mounted on you, he can have the first hand in your collar, it is the second hand that you have to avoid. Conversely when you are attacking someone the first hand needs to go in as deeply and as well as possible because when you get your second hand grip may be more difficult to get and especially to adjust as your opponent will be set on preventing that grip from occurring.

When you choke someone there are two options he either taps (submits) or he sleeps. Not tapping is easy; not sleeping is a different story. The secret of the choke is in the adjustment, when you roll your wrist. After that when I pull the elbows in then you either tap or sleep!

When I defend I take away whatever the opponent wants to get, conversely I know exactly what I need to get in order to succeed.

My favorite submission is the choke, (figure 16) because the choke defeats even the brave, the choke you simply pass out. The two arteries are easy to reach and press down on making it easy to apply. I have always preferred the choke and won most of my fights via choke. It is important to get a deep grip and when you pull to turn the wrists as if you are wringing the hand so that the thumbs come together and touch each other, then I pull the elbows towards myself, pulling his head to my chest.

FIGURE 16

What is the secret of getting a submission?

It is the ability to observe the exact moment that your opponent commits a mistake and take advantage of it. The secret is always to wait for your opponent to expose himself for the right submission. Every submission has a proper time and set up that needs to be present for it to be successful.

What do you think when you get in a submission position?

It depends, if I catch him in a choke my thought is he is going to sleep.

What is your philosophy of fighting?

You need to enter a fight not to lose.

What is the most important thing for a new or beginning Jiu-Jitsu practitioner?
He needs to find an instructor who can teach him the Jiu-Jitsu that he is looking
for so he can fulfill his necessities.

What can you do to get better technically besides having a good teacher?
You need to always look for the way to execute a position so that the use of power
is the last element for success. You need to look for the leverage points so you can
execute the move effortlessly without needing to use power. The use of physical
power to correct a flaw always leads to the incorrect application of the proper technique. Power gets in the way of learning

***You always fought bigger and stronger opponents, generally without rules. Why
    did you do that?***
First I wanted to test myself. I was a light and weak person, I fought against bigger
guys, so I had to develop a style in which the weak person could practice and use
the Jiu-Jitsu. In my style of Jiu-Jitsu, the weak person has an advantage in learning
it and in using it. A normal fight depends on the use of power and what happens
if you don't have the power to match your opponent's power? You lose.

Do you have a philosophy of life?
I wrote a book about the moral aspects of humans. No one really knows himself,
there are 58 moral aspects and you don't even know and use 10 to survive, you
need intelligence, courage, ability etc. May be 10 at most but how about when
another situation occurs that you are asked to dig into the others aspects? How are
you going to behave them? There are people that say afterwards, if I only knew I
wouldn't have done it! Nothing happens by chance and no one gets what he doesn't
deserve everything you get good or bad is deserved! Nature is not evil or unjust if
something bad happens to you it is because you deserved it. No one gets what he
doesn't deserve, everything you get, whether good or bad is deserved. Everything I
get good or bad I thank God for it.

   To those who have the opportunity to read what I have written, I declare that I
am not trying to correct or reprehend anyone. It is what I think and how I see
myself. Please take into account that I am a primary man and ignorant although I
am not that stupid! If there is a notion that a person of culture ignores, it is because
they will only learn when they get to be my age and have time to think about
things.

   Courage is one of the most important qualities in the human being. The person
with courage is a calm human being because nothing bothers him. The courage
that I refer to is the one where the citizen strong, weak, rich or poor defends his
rights and points of view that he believes in without fear.

   I was once asked how I interpret fear. I reply that fear is a state of mind where a
person fears death as if anyone has ever been able to life without dying in the end.
I can however give my opinion about fear such as fearing lions, snakes, dogs, cats
etc. I reference to that fear with the proper precautions taken one can enter a dan-

gerous animal habitat without anything happening. If I go to Africa and I am not properly prepared I will get eaten alive.

Without perseverance you cannot get anywhere in life!

There is nothing more rewarding than being deserving of someone's confidence. Because when you lose someone's confidence it becomes very hard to reacquire it.

You can only have conviction if you believe what you preach!

If you are lazy you are beaten and don't know it and when you find out it may be too late to change.

Do you have any final thoughts you'd like to share?

At my age I am getting forgetful, I may forget names of my relatives and even names of friends but I don't forget the Jiu-Jitsu.

The Team

Grandmaster Helio Gracie

Helio Gracie was born in Belém, Brazil on October 1, 1913, the youngest son of Gastão and Cesalina Gracie's eight children. Throughout his childhood years Helio, affectionately known as "Caxinguele" to his family and friends, was always a frail kid prone to fainting spells. Young Helio's fainting spells and his frailty were such a factor that after a few years he had to forgo going to school, staying home instead. While staying home, Helio would watch his older brother Carlos teach the Jiu-Jitsu that he had learned from a Japanese immigrant called Count Koma. One day, Carlos was late for class and young Helio offered to teach the class to the awaiting student, who, knowing Helio's history of lack of physical skills, jokingly accepted. At the end of the lesson Carlos arrived hurriedly, but the student had been conquered and asked Carlos, if he wouldn't mind, if he could continue having lessons with Helio instead. The surprised Carlos agreed and the legendary career of Helio Gracie began.

In the following years, Helio would modify, improve and evolve the traditional Japanese Jiu-Jitsu so much that a new martial was born called Gracie Jiu-Jitsu. Helio's lack of physical skills forced him to introduce the concepts of leverage, transition and positioning to make up for the physical demands of the traditional martial art. Nephew Carlos Gracie Jr. puts it: "Helio is a genius who dedicated forty years of his life to perfect and advance Jiu-Jitsu. He perfected the leverages and sharpened the techniques." Helio became the head instructor of the Gracie Jiu-Jitsu Academy in Rio de Janeiro, where they taught over 600 classes per week. Many of Helio's students became influential teachers themselves, helping spread the seeds of Jiu-Jitsu. In addition to his sons, Helio taught alongside other great instructors like Carlson, Rolls, and Carlos Jr,

Encouraged by his brother Carlos, his mentor and who he considered to be like a father, Helio's prowess in the martial art led him to a career in professional fighting as a way to test his newly developed technical modifications. Helio's success in the rings with a career of 26 years and over sixteen fights against fighters from around the globe, including the man considered the greatest Jiu-Jitsu fighter Japan ever produced: master Masahiko Kimura. He also took part in the longest fight in history, a 3 hour and 45 minute battle against a former student, 20 years younger and 66 pounds heavier, called Waldemar Santana, which gave him enormous exposure and fame in his native Brazil. Helio was considered to be a national hero as attested by countless articles in the national newspapers and even a book, *Helio Gracie, A Brazilian Superman,* written by notable journalist Jose Amadio, then director of National Magazine *O Cruzeiro.*

Helio Gracie fathered nine children: his seven sons Rorion, Relson, Rickson, Rolker, Royler, Royce and Robin, and two daughters, Rherika and Ricci. Every one of his sons became influential instructors and fighters throughout the world.

In his lifetime of dedication and sacrifice Helio Gracie created a martial art and a legacy that spread around the world and touched and influenced the lives of thousands.

At 93 years old, Helio Gracie still teaches and practices the art that he created in his home in Itaipava, a suburb in the mountains around Rio de Janeiro.

Royler Gracie

The name Royler Gracie is synonymous with competition and teaching. Royler began his competition career as a six year old. During his early years he was already winning titles and collecting medals. A chip off the old block, Royler, with his father the Grandmaster's incentive, always strove to be the best and to have fun in competition. His quest to be the best culminated in 1996 when he won the first of his then unprecedented four consecutive World Jiu-Jitsu titles.

Royler returned to claim another world title in 1997, but wasn't satisfied with just the featherweight title this time. Knowing that a 143-pounder could only go so far in the absolute division, he still entered, fighting a 275-pounder in the first round. Royler defeated him with ease. He went on to defeat another 200-pounder before finally losing to the equally large world champion in the semifinal. His awe-inspiring performance earned him the Most Technical Fighter award. In his decades of fighting, Royler Gracie became the symbol of competition and one of the most intense jiu-jitsu practitioners ever to don a gi.

Testing himself against the best Jiu-Jitsu fighters in the world wasn't enough for Royler, which led him to venture to other arenas. Competing against fighters from other grappling arts and without the use of the gi, Royler participated in the ADCC World Submission Wrestling event and again proved to be the best winning the title three consecutive years from 1998 to 2000 winning the Most Technical award in '98 and becoming the first person ever to win the World BJJ title and the World Submission title in the same year. Royler also ventured in Mixed Martial Arts fighting where he competed and secured a winning record in some of the biggest events on earth: Pride, K-1 and Rumble on The Rock. Now, at age forty, with a storied career behind him, Royler is still one of the most influential and sought-out teachers in jiu-jitsu.

To understand what makes Royler a superb instructor, take a look at that list of Most Technical Fighter awards. Royler has spent much of his career defeating larger—sometimes much larger—men in the mats and rings. The intensity and the will to win are factors, but they come from within, and can be hard to translate from instructor to student. Royler's love of teaching allows him to instill his techniques and spirit in his students.

Royler holds down his duties as academy instructor and top-notch competitor while being father to four daughters. Royler takes his role as father seriously—as he does his surfing hobby, and his projects to help needy children in Rio de Janeiro.

Kid Peligro

One of the leading martial arts writers in the world, Kid Peligro is responsible for regular columns in *Gladiator* and *Gracie Magazine*, as well as one of the most widely read Internet MMA news page, *ADCC News*. He has been the author or coauthor of an unprecedented string of bestsellers in recent years, including *The Gracie Way*, *Brazilian Jiu-Jitsu: Theory and Technique*, *Brazilian Jiu-Jitsu Self-Defense Techniques*, *Brazilian Jiu-Jitsu Black Belt Techniques*, *Brazilian Jiu-Jitsu Submission Grappling Techniques*, and *The Essential Guard*. A 2nd Degree black belt in Jiu-Jitsu who trains with the world's best, Kid is considered to be on the cutting edge of technical knowledge. His broad involvement in the martial arts has led him to travel to the four corners of the earth as an ambassador for the sport that changed his life. He makes his home in San Diego.

Ricardo Azoury

Ricardo Azoury has been involved with Jiu-Jitsu all of his life. One of the original students of Rolls Gracie, Ricardo's passion for the sport only was surpassed by his passion for photography. Considered one of the best photographers in Brazil, Ricardo's eye for movement and composition and his understanding of Jiu-Jitsu have made him one of the top photographers in the sport. Ricardo has been involved in every book that Royler has produced, including the first and ground-breaking *Brazilian Jiu-Jitsu Theory and Technique*. Ricardo's photos have been instrumental in revealing Royler's teachings to his readers.

The Assistants

Helping Royler demonstrate his techniques are two of his top instructors:

David Adiv

David Adiv started his journey into martial arts in his native Israel. David began learning Judo at the age of five and won local, national, and international championships, receiving his black belt at age sixteen. After discovering Brazilian Jiu-Jitsu in 1990, David started to train under Royler in 1992. David received all his belts from Royler, and was awarded his black belt in 2000.

David accompanied Royler and Rickson Gracie for Royler's first Vale-Tudo match in Japan in 1995, and has traveled with Royler as a training partner and cornerman in every major match since. He has competed in two Pan-American championships, taking second place both times, and also competed in the first Rickson Gracie International Tournament, where he not only won his division but also walked away with the award for the most technical fighter.

Wellington "Megaton" Dias

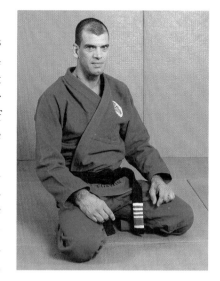

Megaton was born and raised in Rio de Janeiro, Brazil, starting his martial arts training when he was five years old. He achieved his judo black belt rank in 1984 and was Rio state champion. While training and competing in Judo, Megaton met Royler Gracie. Royler invited him to train at the Gracie Academy. He trained under Royler, Rolker, and Rickson Gracie, eventually receiving his black belt at the age of eighteen from Royler. He has since had the opportunity to train with some of the best Olympic athletes and coaches in the world.

Megaton finished second in the BJJ World Championships in 1995, and third in 1999, 2000, and 2001. He won the Pan-American title in 1998, 2000, and 2001 and was the gold medalist in the Fourth International BJJ Championship in 2002. He also won the Rickson Gracie International Championship in 1997 and 2000, winning the most technical fighter award as well. In 2006 Megaton captured the World Master's Title. Megaton lives in Phoenix, Arizona, where he directs the Megaton Brazilian Jiu-Jitsu Academy.

1. Choke from standing

Grandmaster Helio Gracie believes in having solid grips for his submissions, especially the chokes. As the Grandmaster says, "If your hands grip properly, the submission is almost complete." Many times, when fighting for grip control your opponent will concentrate so much on the battle for control that he leaves himself open for a choke. In this case, fighting the stand-up battle, both fighters exchange grips until one gets the advantage. The grip switches from collar to sleeve and back to collar as they fight for control. Whenever he is able to use his right hand to control the inside of his opponent's collar, Grandmaster Helio likes to use this choke as a quick fight ender.

1 Royler and Helio fight for grip control while standing. They both have similar grips. Helio's right hand holds Royler's left collar and his left hand controls Royler's right sleeve at the elbow.

2 Helio quickly changes his grip, using his right hand on the inside of Royler's right lapel. In order to maximize his success it is very important for Helio to slide his hand as far up on the collar as possible. Royler is still concerned with the battle for grip control and does not sense the danger of the grip.

3 Helio releases his left hand from Royler's right sleeve and slides it under his own right arm to grab the inside of Royler's left lapel with the fingers in and the thumb out. Again Helio slides his hand as far up the collar as possible. Note: There are two ways for the second hand to grip the collar. This one, with the fingers in and the thumb out is Helio's favorite but they will demonstrate the other way later.

4 With both hands securely grabbing the collar, Helio tightens the choke by twisting his wrists in while pulling them towards his chest, thus bringing his elbows close to his sides. Notice that for greatest choking pressure Helio brings Royler's head close to the center of his chest.

2. Kimura from standing

Grandmaster Helio believes you should always take the first available opportunity to finish a fight, whether by submission or otherwise. The stand-up battle offers many opportunities as fighters vie for grip control in order to achieve a takedown. In this case Royler secures a very defensive grip with his left hand on Helio's belt and his arm extended to both maintain distance and control Helio's hips. This prevents Helio from pulling guard or bringing the hips in for a takedown attempt. With Royler's arm extended and the hand locked in defense, Grandmaster sees the opportunity for the kimura and takes it.

1 Helio and Royler are facing each other fighting for control. Royler secures a right hand grip (with the fingers pointing up) on Helio's belt. Controlling the center always gives you an advantage in any fight; in this case Royler's control over Helio's belt controls both their distance and Helio's ability to move his hips. Helio has the standard grip with his right hand on Royler's left collar and his left hand grabbing Royler's right sleeve just below the elbow.

2 Helio slides his left hand down along Royler's right arm until he reaches his wrist. Helio presses the wrist against his hips, locking Royler's hand in place. Helio then steps forward with his right leg so his foot lands between Royler's feet. He loops his right arm over Royler's right arm, grapevining it until he can lock his right hand onto his own left wrist, securing the figure-4 grip for the kimura. Notice that Helio's torso is bent forward with the hips pushed back slightly in order to reach around Royler's arm and secure the lock.

3 Helio extends his body, driving his hips forward and using the power of his entire body to break Royler's grip on his belt and drive his right arm around towards his back for the kimura lock. Notice that the torque is a circular motion with Helio driving Royler's wrist in a clockwise direction as if he wanted to force Royler's right wrist to reach Royler's own right ear.

3. Takedown to foot-lock (same side leg)

Grandmaster Helio is fond of all submissions. He believes that as long as they get the opponent to submit they are all his favorites. Many practitioners shy away from foot-locks, but Helio believes they are an especially effective way to finish the fight. Foot-locks are not often applied from the stand-up battle, and this unique application makes this takedown especially effective.

1 Helio and Royler are in a stand-up clinch, both grabbing each other's left collar with the right hand and the right elbow with the left hand.

2 Sensing a slight give in Royler's right arm tension, Helio attacks. First he drops his hips and steps the right foot forward between Royler's feet to bring his hips closer to Royler for better leverage. Helio then bends down to grab Royler's right leg behind the knee with his left hand. Helio straightens his legs, raising his body up while pulling Royler's right leg off the ground. At the same time he drives his right hand forward against Royler's chest to push him back. Royler is driven off balance, with the weight of his body on his left leg. Notice that Helio wraps his left arm around Royler's right leg at the knee.

3 Helio circles his right leg around the inside of Royler's left leg. He kicks the right foot forward and then draws it back using his heel to strike the back of Royler's left heel, tripping him. At the same time Helio pushes forward with his right arm forcing Royler's chest back and causing him to fall backwards. As Royler hits the ground, Helio slides his left arm up towards Royler's right ankle. He locks his left hand onto his own right wrist while placing his right hand on Royler's right shinbone for the figure-4 lock on the foot. Helio's right leg is between Royler's legs with his shin pressing down on Royler's left thigh to prevent Royler from using the leg to counter the lock by kicking up or pushing against Helio's chest to break the grip. With Royler's right foot held in his armpit, Helio applies the foot-lock by leaning back while driving the hips forward. He uses his back to push Royler's toes back as his figure-4 lock applies pressure on the ankle joint.

3 DETAIL: Notice Helio's figure-4 grip on Royler's ankle: the left forearm is right under the Achilles tendon as close to the heel as possible. The left hand grabs the right wrist and the right hand rests on top of Royler's right shinbone. Note that both hands have all five fingers together in a claw. It is very important for Helio to cinch the noose around Royler's ankle very tightly before he initiates the submission move. Otherwise he risks losing control of the foot; for instance, Royler's heel may slip from the noose sliding over the top of Helio's left forearm.

4. Choke from the mount

The choke from the mounted position is one of Grandmaster Helio's favorite finishing holds. The keys to successfully applying the choke from the mount are, first, to maintain the position and second, to apply and maintain the proper choking pressure.

1 Helio is mounted on Royler. He has proper position with his knees semi-close but not tight against Royler's side and his hips are slightly up on Royler's chest. Helio's back is straight and his eyes look down on the target: Royler's neck.

2 Helio slides his left hand inside Royler's left collar. His fingers reach the inside while the thumb stays on the outside. Seeking to secure the best possible grip for the choke, Helio slides the hand as far back on Royler's collar as possible. Notice that Helio is not leaning forward with his torso as he seeks stability to maintain the position. Otherwise, if he were to lean forward, it would be easier for Royler to escape with a bridge and roll.

Finishing your opponent from the mounted position

In a street fight or a Gracie Jiu-Jitsu match, the mount is one of the best positions to be in. From there you can strike or apply most of the finishing holds available in the art. The mount, however, is also one of the hardest positions to maintain because there are so many escapes available to your opponent. To successfully finish from the mounted position one needs first to maintain the position. By defusing your opponent's escape attempts and maintaining the mount you will induce your opponent to panic and struggle harder and harder to escape, giving you opportunities to apply the finishing holds.

Grandmaster believes very strongly that the basic positions are the keys to everything. Simplicity is the master:

"Jiu-Jitsu is a circle that some of us transform into a circus. We go and try more advanced and complicated options (the circus). But at the end of the circle we come back to the simple basic position." In general, submissions are linked one to another and to another. As your opponent counters your first attack, you quickly seek another opening and use the next attack option; if he is successful at defending the next attack, you immediately switch to the next option in your chain. The greater the series of submissions you have linked together, the greater the chance you have to submit your opponent. Each switch gives you an edge by controlling the timing of the fight and increasing your chances of success.

3 Helio turns his shoulders to his left and reaches with his right hand to grab Royler's right collar. Having secured the grips on both collars, Helio rings his arms together and gets ready to apply the choke.

3 DETAIL: Notice the hand grip. Helio reaches with the thumb inside and the fingers outside the collar. This is the second hand grip option; it is a quicker way to secure the collar grip, and speed may be very important as you are trying to both secure the finishing hold and maintain the position at the same time.

4 Helio applies the choking pressure by bringing his wrists and forearms together and drawing the elbows up toward his chest as he leans forward. The elbows do not open out during the choking motion. Using only the forearm muscles to choke would actually deliver less pressure than pulling the elbows up and expanding the chest, allowing you to use the bigger back muscles to apply the choking pressure.

5. Key-lock (Americana) from the mount

Many times, when mounted, an opponent will keep his arms in front of his chest and neck to protect against chokes and punches. In that case the key-lock is the perfect attack. The keys for the key-lock are to maintain your weight pressure on the wrist so the opponent cannot straighten his arm out and to keep his wrist sliding on the ground as you apply the submission. At times to get the right opening for the key-lock Helio may feign a choke attack, drawing the opponent's arms up to defend, and then switch to the key-lock.

1 Helio is mounted on Royler. Royler has his arms and hands in front of his chest and neck to protect from punches and to prevent Helio from choking him. Helio holds Royler's forearms with his hands leaning slightly forward to apply his weight to the arms.

2 Helio decides to attack Royler's left arm. He turns his shoulders to his right, grabs Royler's left wrist with his left hand (thumb pointing down) and uses the twisting motion of his torso and his weight to drive Royler's wrist to the mat. It is very important for Helio to use his weight and not just the power of his arms to drive Royler's wrist to the mat, especially when fighting against a much larger and stronger opponent.

3 Having pinned Royler's left wrist to the mat, Helio slides his right hand under Royler's left arm until he can grab his own left wrist with his right hand to secure the figure-4 lock around Royler's arm. Notice that Helio has his left elbow tight against Royler's left ear and puts some of his weight on that elbow. This is a very important detail; by doing that Helio has more power to prevent Royler from straightening his arm to defend the key-lock. Also notice Helio's hand grip: the hand grabs over the wrist with the four fingers gripping the top of the wrist with the thumb grabbing the bottom. Helio's thumbs are pointing towards his own elbows.

4 Helio applies the key-lock by turning his shoulders further to his right, sliding Royler's wrist down on the mat towards his knee. At the same time Helio raises his right elbow up, torquing Royler's left arm around the shoulder joint.

6. Arm-lock from the mount

A common counter to the key-lock attack is for the opponent to turn towards the wrist in jeopardy and use his opposite arm to try to pull it back to prevent it from being pinned to the mat. In that case the arm-lock from the mount is a perfect option. Notice that these three attacks are perfectly linked together. As the opponent reacts, Grandmaster Helio can switch between all three.

1 Helio is mounted on Royler looking to attack. Royler holds Helio's arms to prevent Helio from choking him.

2 Helio decides to attack Royler's left arm with the key-lock and turns his shoulder to the right. He grabs Royler's wrist and forearm and drives it to the mat. Sensing the upcoming key-lock attack, Royler quickly counters as he turns to his own left, reaching with his right hand and grabbing his left hand to prevent Helio from pinning it to the mat. Helio has anticipated Royler's counter and is not taken by surprise. Helio sees Royler's exposed his right arm and switches to attack it with an arm-lock. He slides the left knee up towards Royler's head and presses his chest against Royler's right arm, trapping it and preventing Royler from pulling it back to the mat.

3 While still fighting to pin Royler's left wrist to the mat, Helio uses his hands as pivot points. He puts his weight on the hands, making his legs and hips light and allowing him to pivot his body to his left. He further slides the left knee up towards Royler's head and drives his hips forward, pressing against the right shoulder. Helio steps over Royler's head with his left leg, the foot landing in front of the face, preventing Royler from circling his body to his left to escape the attack.

4 Helio wraps his left arm around Royler's right arm and sits back down on the mat right next to Royler's body. He makes sure his hips are still tight against the arm, taking away any space through which Royler might attempt to pull the right elbow. Helio leans back and extends his body and Royler's right arm and drives his hips up against the elbow joint, hyper-extending it for the arm-lock. Notice Helio's thighs are pressing into Royler's arm and his heel pushes down on the ground so he can apply pressure with the back of his legs on Royler's face and torso to prevent him from escaping. Since this is a fast arm-lock, Helio quickly reacts to Royler's counter. He doesn't secure the grip on Royler's right arm and then slowly and deliberately execute the arm-lock — this would alert Royler to the new impending attack and give him the opportunity to try to counter it — but rather surprises him with his quick spin over the head and arm extension.

7. Neck-crank from side control

This is perhaps Grandmaster Helio's trademark technique. Over his lifetime he has caught many opponents with this submission. In his philosophy of submission Grandmaster Helio likes to state: "I don't try to get what I want, instead I take whatever the opponent gives me." The opportunity to apply this neck-crank occurs every time your opponent raises his head from the mat to escape the side-control position (a very common reaction). Take advantage of the moment and you will be surprised how effective the submission is.

1 Helio has side-control on Royler. Helio has both arms on Royler's left side; his left elbow is tight against Royler's left ear and his right elbow presses against Royler's hip. Royler has good defensive posture with his right arm curled and the forearm braced against Helio's hip while his left hand is under Helio's right armpit.

2 As Royler pushes off his feet and turns to his right to escape from side-control, Helio immediately wraps his left arm around Royler's neck and holds his own right lapel with the hand.

2 DETAIL: Notice Helio's left hand holding his right lapel with the arm wrapped tight around Royler's neck. It is very important for Helio to have a tight noose around Royler's neck; otherwise the head may escape as he tries to add the pressure.

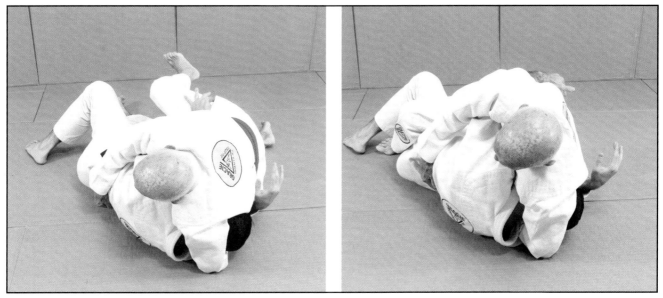

3 As Royler continues to struggle to turn to his right and escape from the bottom Helio turns his hips to his right, sliding the left knee under his body. He grabs Royler's belt with his right hand to both prevent his hips from escaping and to help loop his right leg over Royler's legs and lock his calf on Royler's left thigh.

4 Grandmaster then arches his body back, thrusting his hips forward and pressing Royler's head down with his left arm for the neck-crank submission.

8. Reverse arm-lock from the guard

Grandmaster Helio has many variations of the arm-lock from the guard, this being one of his favorites. The move begins much like an omoplata, or shoulder lock, but Helio switches to the reverse arm-lock because it is quicker and requires less commitment on his part, allowing him to quickly switch to a variety of other attacks rather than being locked in the omoplata.

1 Royler is inside Helio's guard with his hands pressing on Helio's biceps to block any chokes and other attacks.

2 Helio's first step in any attack from the guard is to break down Royler's defensive posture. He does that by using his legs to pull Royler's torso forward while circling his forearms under Royler's arms. He uses the circular motion to collapse Royler's brace on the biceps, breaking his posture.

3 Helio escapes his hips slightly to his left as he wraps his left arm around Royler's right arm. Notice that Helio grabs Royler's right sleeve just behind the biceps for extra control of the arm. Helio's right hand grabs the back of Royler's left biceps to keep him close.

4 Helio plants the left foot on the ground and pushes off it to escape the hips further to the left. Helio then moves his torso and head to the left until he has the proper angle to loop his left leg over Royler's right shoulder, locking the heel in front of Royler's face. Helio slides his left hand down Royler's arm so his hand pushes down on the elbow. Notice that Helio's right leg is not flat on the ground but rather raised with the calf locked on Royler's left hip so he cannot move to his right or jump over the leg to escape.

5 Helio continues to turn his body to the left until he is approximately perpendicular to Royler. At this point he presses his knees together, forcing his left leg tight against Royler's right arm and trapping it completely. He thrusts his hips forward, pressing against Royler's right elbow and applying great pressure on the joint for the submission.

6 Should Royler manage to pull his wrist out to escape the pressure, Helio can grab Royler's right wrist with both hands and pull the arm back against his hips and left thigh, forcing the elbow against his thigh to hyper-extend the joint for the reverse arm-lock. Notice that Helio makes sure Royler's thumb points up as this assures him that the elbow is locked and pointing back.

9. Arm-wrap collar choke from the guard

An optional attack from the guard is the arm-wrap choke. It can either be executed directly or as a counter when the opponent leans towards the trapped arm to defend it and try to pry it out. In that case Grandmaster simply adjusts to the opponent's reaction and goes for the choke.

1 Royler is inside Helio's guard with his hands pressing on Helio's biceps to block any chokes and attacks.

2 Helio circles his forearms under Royler's arms, using the circular motion to break Royler's brace on his biceps. Helio escapes his hips slightly to his own left as he wraps his left arm around Royler's right arm. This time however Royler leans to his right, preventing Helio from looping the left leg over the arm.

3 Helio takes advantage of Royler's reaction and switches to the choke; he plants the feet down and pushes off, thrusting his hips up slightly to create space between himself and Royler. At the same time, he slides the left hand between his chest and Royler's chest, fully circling Royler's right arm. Helio uses the right hand to feed Royler's left collar to his left hand.

4 Helio turns his torso to his left and loops the right arm over Royler's head so he can lock his left hand (thumb in and fingers out) on the right side of the collar just behind the head. Helio then circles the right elbow over Royler's head until the forearm is under the neck. He applies the choking pressure for the submission by pulling down on the left collar with his left hand and raising the right elbow up, tightening the right collar and pushing the forearm against Royler's throat.

10. Arm-lock from standing against the sit up guard

Often times a guard player will sit facing the opponent and fight from what is commonly referred as the "sit up" guard (using his front arm to pull on the opponent's gi and the legs to trip or attack him with a submission). Grandmaster Helio has the perfect answer for this situation with this arm-lock.

1 Helio stands in front of Royler. Royler has his left arm back bracing his torso and his right leg forward and up in the classic sit up guard posture. Royler pulls on Helio's gi collar with the right arm. Helio grabs Royler's right sleeve at the wrist with his right hand and at the triceps with his left hand and pulls it back, resisting Royler's grip.

2 Maintaining the tension on the grip, Helio steps forward between Royler's legs close to the groin with his right foot and pulls Royler's arm up. Notice that Helio's right foot is parallel to Royler's chest.

3 Helio leans slightly back with his torso while continuing to pull Royler's right arm back. He loops his left leg over Royler's head until his hips press against the back of Royler's right elbow.

4 Helio lands his left foot on the mat next to Royler's left thigh and arches his torso back while driving his hips forward against Royler's right elbow, hyper-extending it. Notice that just prior to completing the arm-lock Helio transfers the left-hand grip from Royler's triceps to the wrist. He waits for the last moment to transition to the wrist to prevent Royler from pulling his arm back and out of the lock.

11. Arm-lock from side-control bottom

Gracie Jiu-Jitsu is an art in which a person can defend himself and even excel from positions that are normally associated with defeat. Being able to defend oneself and even fight from the bottom is one of its greatest advantages. The side-control bottom position is usually a defensive position, but Grandmaster Helio has a few tricks to use from this position. He takes advantage of his opponent's attempt to maintain control and defend the escape to finish the fight with this arm-lock.

1 Royler has side-control on Helio. Royler's right elbow presses against Helio's left hip, and his right knee presses on the right hip, taking away Helio's mobility. Royler's left elbow is tight against Helio's left ear, keeping Helio's head in place to prevent him from escaping from the bottom. Helio has his right elbow and forearm blocking Royler's hips to create the space for his possible escape

2 Helio pushes off his left foot and turns his body to his right as he escapes the hip back. Helio's left hand grabs Royler's right wrist, controlling the arm and setting up the submission.

3 Helio begins to replace the guard by sliding the right knee in front of Royler's hips, blocking him from getting close and re-establishing the side-control. Helio pushes off with his right knee and drives his torso to his left (counter-clockwise) moving his head away from Royler so he cannot control the head. Helio has his right arm on Royler's chest to keep him away.

4 Helio continues moving his torso to his left and loops the left leg over Royler's head, making sure to keep his thigh tight against Royler's right arm. Helio locks his thigh over Royler's right shoulder keeping the calf in front of Royler's face. He turns his body to his right, locking Royler's right arm with both legs. He slides his hands to Royler's wrist and extends his legs and arches his torso back, driving his hips against Royler's elbow for the arm-lock.

12. Arm-lock from the guard

Another classic submission is the arm-lock from the guard. Although it is a very effective stand-alone submission, the arm-lock from the guard is even more successful when used in conjunction with a choke attempt. The opponent's reaction in countering the choke will yield the best opportunity for the arm-lock finish. Grandmaster Gracie uses a fierce choke to set-up the arm-lock.

1 Helio has Royler in his closed guard. Helio makes sure his first grip (with the right hand) is solid and deep, setting up the choke. Royler defends the choke using his right arm, with the hand over Helio's left biceps to prevent the second hand, in this case Helio's left hand, from reaching his collar and completing the choke.

2 Helio continues trying for the choke as he prepares the secondary attack: the arm-lock. Pushing off with his right foot, Helio escapes his hips to his left and places his left foot on Royler's right hip to try to free the left arm. His goal is to reach the collar for the choke by looping it up and around Royler's right hand block. Royler maintains his defense by extending the right arm and using the hand to follow Helio's arm as it moves. Royler's defense makes him vulnerable to the arm-lock and Helio immediately takes advantage of the opening.

3 Helio wraps his left arm around Royler's right wrist, trapping it in place. Pushing off his right calf, Helio lifts his hips and loops the left leg over Royler's head, locking the calf over the left side of Royler's face.

4 Helio completes the arm-lock by securing Royler's right wrist and forearm with his hands as he drives his calves down. He pushes off Royler's head and side to help lift his hips up against Royler's right elbow, hyper-extending it for the submission. Note that Helio's calves pushing down on Royler accomplish two things: they help him lift his hips up while at the same time they keep Royler away and off-balance. This prevents Royler from countering the arm-lock by leaning forward and stacking Helio.

13. Mata-leao, or rear naked choke

When it comes to submissions, Grandmaster Helio says that he will take whatever the opponent gives him. If given the choice, however, he would certainly prefer the choke. The Grandmaster believes that chokes are the best submissions, better than joint locks. As he puts it: "If you are tough, you can fight with a broken arm, but you can't fight when you are choked out!" Of all the chokes, the mata-leao ("lion killer") or rear naked choke is perhaps Gracie Jiu-Jitsu's most famous; it is powerful, effective and relatively easy to apply. Because of all this, the mata-leao is an outstanding way for a Gracie Jiu-Jitsu fighter to finish a fight and its use generally indicates complete mastery of the opponent.

1 Helio is on Royler's back. He has legs wrapped around Royler's waist, his calves over the top of Royler's thighs, and the heels, used as hooks, pressed against the thighs. Royler is prevented from moving his hips and escaping the back control.

2 Helio twists his shoulders to his left and attacks with his right arm, wrapping it around Royler's neck until his hand is over Royler's left shoulder and the elbow is centered in front of Royler's neck.

3 Helio bends the left arm and brings it towards his right. He locks his right hand over his left biceps and places the left hand, with the palm facing forward, behind Royler's head to complete the lock.

4 Helio applies the choking pressure by bringing his elbows together, expanding his chest, and pulling his arm in towards his chest, pressing Royler's neck with his arms for the submission.

4 DETAIL: Notice Helio's form on the choke: his elbow is centered in front of Royler's neck, the right hand grabs over the left biceps and the left hand, palm facing forward, presses the back of Royler's head. The choking pressure is in and not up, as if Helio was trying to squeeze Royler's neck between his arms in a motion similar to hugging a long lost friend.

14. Choke from standing, jumps to guard

Royler here demonstrates a variation on his father's choke from standing. The situation is the same. Royler and Megaton fight for the grip advantage and Royler takes advantage of the moment to slip his choke in. This time, however, he jumps to guard, adding even more pressure to the choke.

1 Royler and Megaton exchange grips trying to get an advantage for a takedown.

2 Royler pivots on his feet and turns his hips and shoulders to his right. Royler's right hand pulls open Megaton's left lapel making it easy for him to slip the left hand deep in the collar. Notice that Royler uses the standard grip (four fingers in and the thumb out).

3 Royler pushes off his feet again and pivots to the left, sliding the right hand under the left arm and grabbing Megaton's right collar, securing the choke.

4 Royler jumps to guard, with his legs wrapped around Megaton's waist and his feet interlocked behind his back. He pulls the choke tight by bringing his chest up towards Megaton's head. Royler further tightens the choke by bringing the wrists together and twisting them in towards his chest as he expands his chest and brings his elbows back.

15. Wrist-lock from the standing grip battle 1

Many times in the fight for grips, opponents get so caught up in the exchanges and their quest to control the center that they forget about certain dangers, such as this wrist-lock. This is one quick and effective fight ender as the wrist pain is tremendous. Be careful when practicing this with your partner!

1 Royler and Megaton exchange grips standing. Megaton's right wrist grabs Royler's left collar near the centerline of the chest. Royler pushes Megaton's right forearm in, forcing the wrist to bend in. Megaton can either release the grip or face the wrist-lock.

2 Royler quickly slides his left hand down Megaton's arm toward his wrist as he twists his torso to the right, locking Megaton's hand on his chest near the right shoulder.

3 Royler grabs Megaton's right elbow with his right hand, locking the arm in place. At this point Megaton cannot release his arm from Royler's control.

4 Royler grabs the back of his own right hand with his left hand, curls his shoulders in and pulls Megaton's elbow in towards his chest to apply the wrist lock.

4 DETAIL: Notice the wrist-lock: Megaton's right wrist is locked on to Royler's chest. Royler pulls Megaton's elbow towards his chest; Royler's chest forces Megaton's fingers back towards the elbow causing the hand to bend back on the wrist for the lock.

16. Wrist-lock from the standing grip battle 2

At times your opponent may grip your gi high on your collar near your far shoulder, preventing you from applying the previous wrist-lock In that case, this wrist-lock option is a better choice.

1 Royler and Megaton exchange grips standing. Megaton's right wrist grabs Royler's left collar high near the left shoulder. The wrist-lock used in technique 15 will not work because Megaton's arm is not positioned properly, so Royler opts for this variation.

2 Royler immediately grabs the back of Megaton's right elbow with his left hand as he turns his shoulder in and to his right, locking Megaton's wrist in place. At the same time Royler strikes Megaton's right wrist in with his right hand, forcing it to buckle out.

2 DETAIL: Notice how Royler strikes Megaton's right wrist with his right hand causing it to buckle out; the wrist is now trapped by Royler's chest and left shoulder. Megaton cannot pull the arm out since Royler holds the elbow with the left hand.

3 Royler grabs Megaton's elbow with both hands and pulls the arm in as he drives his chest forward forcing the wrist to turn more for the wrist-lock.

17. Wrist-lock from the standing grip battle 3

Royler shows another very effective submission from the standing grip battle here. Remember, you don't have to wait for the fight to go to the ground in order to apply your sub- missions. Often, fighters are so enthralled by the battle for control they actually continue gripping the collar even as you are applying the submission.

1 Royler and Megaton exchange grips while fighting for an advantage. They both have standard grips with one hand on the opponent's collar and the other hand holding the opposite elbow.

2 Royler turns his shoulders to his left and switches his right hand grip from Megaton's left collar to Megaton's right hand, grabbing over the top of the hand.

3 Royler twists his shoulders back to the right as if he is trying to use the motion to break Megaton's grip on his collar. Sensing Royler's intention to break the grip makes Megaton grab Royler's collar even harder. Royler twists Megaton's hand and elbow around in a counter-clockwise direction, exposing Megaton's arm.

4 Royler pivots on his right foot, steps around Megaton's right leg with his left leg and turns his hips and shoulder to his right so his back is to Megaton. At the same time he slides his left hand to the wrist and locks his left arm over Megaton's right arm, trapping it under his armpit. Royler uses his right hand to push Megaton's right wrist in for a wrist-lock. He also pulls the wrist up and drives his armpit against Megaton's elbow for the arm-lock.

4 DETAIL: Notice Royler's hand pushing Megaton's hand back for the wrist-lock.

18. Wrist-lock from the standing grip battle 4

Opportunities for wrist-locks occur all the time in a fight, whether you are on the ground or standing. Royler here demonstrates another wrist-lock using different hand and arm positions than in the previous technique to achieve the same result. Learn the basics of these locks and look to apply similar attacks in different situations.

1 Royler and Megaton are standing in a fight for grip control. Megaton places his right hand on Royler's left biceps, perhaps to block and attack or to maintain arm distance. Regardless, Royler sees the opportunity for a wrist-lock and takes it.

2 Royler immediately bends the left arm in and wraps his left hand over Megaton's right wrist. By bringing the arm in tight, Royler locks Megaton's right hand in the crease of his elbow and prevents him from pulling the hand away.

3 Royler grabs Megaton's right elbow with his right hand.

4 Royler grabs his own right wrist with the left hand, locking a figure-4 around Megaton's right arm, and presses his chest forward. At the same time he turns his shoulders to the right to apply the wrist-lock.

4 DETAIL: Notice Royler's figure-4 around Megaton's right arm. Megaton's hand is trapped in the crease of Royler's left arm. Royler's right hand holds the back of Megaton's right elbow while his left forearm loops over Megaton's right forearm. By turning his shoulders to the right Royler pushes Megaton's hand back, forcing the wrist for the wrist-lock.

19. Arm-lock from the standing grip battle

Another great option for a quick finish from the standing grip battle is shown here. In this case Royler uses an arm wrap to secure control over Megaton's arm.

1 Royler and Megaton exchange grips fighting for an advantage. They both have standard grips: one hand on the opponent's collar and the other hand holding the opposite elbow.

2 Royler arches his torso back as he loops his left arm around Megaton's right arm. Royler bends forward and shoots his left arm up and over Megaton's right arm. Once his elbow is past the arm, Royler drops the elbow down inside Megaton's arm. Notice that Royler drops his torso down as well to make the arm motion much more powerful. This is a very important detail, as it will force the opponent's arm down even if he is very strong. Royler's left arm completes the rotation around Megaton's right arm and locks his hand on Megaton's triceps. Notice how Royler has secured control over Megaton's arm with three elements: his hand grabbing the triceps, the arm wrapped around it and the left shoulder pushing Megaton's forearm down.

3 Royler grabs Megaton's right triceps, placing his right hand just above his left.

4 In one explosive motion Royler steps around Megaton's right leg with his left leg so his foot lands just in front of Megaton's right foot. At the same time Royler rotates his body to his right (clockwise) pulling Megaton's right arm out and over with him.

4 (REVERSE VIEW) Royler's pulling motion causes Megaton to release his grip and his forearm slides on Royler's left arm until the wrist stops on Royler's neck. Royler bends his head to the left and his torso down to block Megaton's wrist from slipping clear of his head. Royler uses both hands to pull Megaton's elbow towards his chest, hyper-extending the elbow for the arm-lock.

20. Standing arm-bar

This standing arm-bar is another one of the surprise positions that work well to quickly finish a fight. Remember that these are advanced positions that need timing and quickness in order for them to work. You must practice them extensively, but don't get discouraged if you don't get immediate results. Perseverance and repetition are keys when trying to master advanced finishing holds. Explosive motion is the critical aspect of this attack and the element you should focus on when you practice.

1 Royler and Megaton face each other in a standard stance.

2 Megaton makes a move to better his control. He reaches with his right hand and grabs Royler's belt behind the back. Royler immediately pivots off his toes and turns his body to his right, dropping the right knee down.

3 Royler continues to pivot and wraps his left arm around Megaton's right forearm and grabs his own left wrist with his right hand.

4 Royler steps forward with his left foot, placing it near Megaton's right foot. He takes a step back with the right foot and makes a big circle with the leg as he quickly and explosively turns his shoulders to the right. This applies intense pressure on Megaton's right elbow. Notice that this is not a smooth controlled move. It is a hard jolt that will both surprise and cause immediate pain to the opponent's joint. Be very careful when practicing it with your partner.

3 DETAIL: Notice Royler's grip: the left arm is wrapped around Megaton's arm with the right hand locked and pulling on his left wrist. Royler keeps all five fingers together.

4 (REVERSE VIEW) Check out Royler's left shoulder and torso movement. The shoulder dips down as the torso spins. Additionally Royler pulls the left arm in with the right hand. The movement is very explosive, creating the jolt on the arm.

21. Loop choke from the standing grip battle

The loop choke is a very solid submission from the standing grip battle and will surprise many opponents, giving you a quick finish for your match. The key to this choke is the set up. Contrary to most chokes, when you want to have the choking hand grab the opponent's collar as high as possible, in the loop choke the hand grabbing the collar cannot be too high and tight up the collar otherwise you will not have enough fabric to loop around the opponent's neck.

1 Royler and Megaton fight for grip control. Royler uses his right hand to grab Megaton's right collar with the fingers positioned in and the thumb out. Notice that Royler's grip is not high, almost behind Megaton's neck, but near the collar bone so he has enough collar for the attack.

2 Royler shakes and brings Megaton down to the ground. He pushes off his toes and lifts his arms to pull Megaton's gi up. Megaton's immediate and natural reaction is to fight back and drop his torso down. Royler explosively pulls Megaton's gi down as he drops to his right knee, causing Megaton to fall to the ground on all fours. Royler's right hand loops Megaton's collar around his neck.

3 Royler shoots his legs back and drives his chest on Megaton's back to keep him from getting back on his feet. Royler wraps his left arm around Megaton's right arm, he slips the hand under the armpit and up and over the back of Megaton's head to set up the choke.

3 DETAIL: Notice how Royler's left arm goes around Megaton's arm. The hand slides under the armpit and then over the back of the head with the palm facing up.

4 Royler drops his left knee to the ground and loops the right leg over as he spins his body in a counter-clockwise direction, forcing Megaton to turn with him. Megaton rolls over Royler, ending up on his back. Royler now has the loop choke on. He reaches with his left hand and grabs Megaton's left armpit, preventing him from releasing the choking pressure by turning to his right. Royler applies the choking pressure by pulling the collar with the right hand while using the left arm to drive Megaton's head up. Note that if Megaton should resist the spin he will be choked by the tremendous pressure of the spin.

22. Takedown to foot-lock (opposite side leg)

Like father, like son, but with a difference! Grandmaster Helio demonstrated his version of the takedown to foot-lock (technique 3) where he attacks the foot on the same side. Royler prefers to reach across and grab the opposite leg, as shown here. Both attacks are equally functional. A matter of opportunity and personal preference determines which one you will use.

1 Royler and Megaton fight for grip control. Both have similar grips on each other with one hand on the collar and the other hand on the sleeve.

2 As they move around, Royler quickly steps forward with his left leg, reaches between Megaton's legs with his left hand and grabs the back of Megaton's left leg (opposite side) just above the knee. Royler steps back wide with his right leg.

3 Royler steps to his left with his right foot lifting Megaton's leg with his arm, forcing him to fall. Notice that the spinning motion of Royler's legs and body cause Megaton to fall.

4 While keeping Megaton's leg up so he can't get up Royler slides his hand to Megaton's ankle and wraps the arm around the ankle tightly near the Achilles tendon and steps forward so Megaton's left leg is between his legs. Royler locks his left hand onto his right wrist for the figure-4 lock around the ankle. Royler thrusts his hips forward and arching the shoulders back applying pressure to the Achilles for the foot-lock.

4 DETAIL: Notice the figure-4 around Megaton's ankle: Royler's left forearm is as tight and as close to the Achilles as possible so Megaton's heel won't escape when Royler applies the pressure. The closer to the heel that the noose is applied, the greater the pressure on the submission.

23. Takedown to knee-lock

Another great attack from the standing position is the take-down to knee-lock. This is a variation of the Ouchi Gari, going to a knee-lock. This is a great combination when you catch the foot—instead of ending up in the guard you launch the next attack, surprising your opponent.

1 Royler and Megaton fight for grip control. Both have similar grips on each other with one hand on the collar and the other hand on the sleeve.

2 Royler commits to the attack by stepping with his right foot just behind Megaton's right heel so the outside edge of his foot touches the mat and the bottom of the foot cups the heel. At the same time Royler grabs the outside of Megaton's right heel with his left hand and drives the right hand into Megaton's chest, pushing him back. Royler continues driving the right hand on Megaton's chest and pulls up on the right ankle with his left hand, bringing the ankle to his left hip, forcing Megaton to fall.

3 Royler keeps control over Megaton's leg by pushing it against his left hip while pressing down on the chest with his right hand to keep Megaton from getting up. Royler slides the right knee over Megaton's groin right next to the right thigh.

4 DETAIL: Notice Royler's legs wrapped and locked around Megaton's right leg. Royler's left leg wraps around Megaton's right leg and hooks the foot under his own right leg behind the knee. Royler's right foot hooks under Megaton's left leg. Notice how Royler's left shin blocks Megaton from turning to his right and getting over the top to escape the lock.

4 Royler closes his left elbow against Megaton's right heel and drives the right knee to the ground as he spins around Megaton's right leg in a counterclockwise direction. Royler ends up on the ground at 90° angle to Megaton's body with his leg extended. Royler locks the figure-4 around Megaton's right leg by wrapping the left leg around and locking the right leg over the left ankle. Royler extends the right leg and hooks his foot under Megaton's left knee and extends his body by thrusting the hips forward against Megaton's knee while using his back to drive Megaton's foot down to the mat, hyper-extending the joint.

24. Flying triangle

The flying triangle is a highly impressive and surprising maneuver that yields surprisingly great results. Opponents never fail to be startled by a flying attack. Although it appears difficult to execute it is actually simple and requires good timing more than flexibility or dexterity. The flying triangle has ended many fights with a quick submission in many tournaments.

1 Royler and Megaton fight for grip control. Both have similar grips on each other with one hand on the collar and the other hand on the sleeve. They have their hips facing out – Royler has his left foot forward and Megaton has his right foot forward. Megaton's right arm is extended and vulnerable, so Royler will focus his attack there.

2 Royler steps further back with the right foot and pulls Megaton down with his arms. Royler jumps up in the air and locks his legs over Megaton's shoulders. The jump: Royler pulls himself up by his hands while driving Megaton's torso down. He pushes off his right foot and steps forward and up with the right leg, then pushes off his left foot. He kicks up the right leg up and over Megaton's left arm and jumps up so his left leg loops over Megaton's right shoulder. Royler's leg movement is as if he was running hurdles.

3 Royler bends his right leg behind Megaton's back and locks the left leg over the right foot for the figure-4 lock around Megaton's right arm and head. Royler's weight forces Megaton to bend forward until his back touches the ground.

4 Royler applies the triangle pressure by bringing his knees together while using both hands to pull the back of Megaton's head forward. Royler's right leg presses on one side of Megaton's neck while Megaton's own right arm presses against the other side, cutting the blood to the head for the choke.

25. Flying arm-lock

Another impressive and quick fight-ending maneuver is the flying arm-lock. The start of the submission is similar to the flying triangle but instead of looping the leg *over* the opponent's arm Royler locks the leg *under* his arm. The submission you use depends on the opponent's posture: if he is crouched lower you use the triangle and the arm-lock if he is standing up straighter.

1 Royler and Megaton fight for grip control. Both have similar grips on each other with one hand on the collar and the other hand on the sleeve. They have their hips facing in and both Royler and Megaton have their right foot forward. Since Megaton's right arm is extended it is vulnerable, Royler will attack Megaton's right arm.

2 In a sudden explosive move Royler pushes off his left foot and shoots his right knee up as he pulls himself by his arms and jumps up, locking his right leg under Megaton's left armpit and loops his left leg over Megaton's head.

3 Royler's weight forces Megaton to bend forward. As Royler's back hits the ground he has pivoted his hips to his right and locked the left calf on the left side of Megaton's head. Royler presses down on Megaton's back with his right calf preventing him from straightening up. Royler's hands grab Megaton's wrist to prevent him from pulling the arm out of the lock. Royler drives his heels down towards the ground, forcing Megaton's head and back down, while at the same time he thrusts his hips up against Megaton's right elbow, hyper-extending the joint for the submission.

3 (SIDEVIEW) Notice how Royler's right calf presses down on Megaton's back to prevent him from raising his torso. Royler will push off that calf to help raise his hips and extend his body for the arm-lock.

26. Arm-lock from standing

The arm-lock from the standing position is another very effective submission that will yield a quick submission. The key to this attack is the surprise factor: you start the movement as if you wanted to pull guard on your opponent by placing your foot on his hip or thigh and dropping your back to the ground, and then quickly switch to the arm-lock.

1 Royler and Megaton are standing fighting for grip control. They have a closed stance, both with their right foot forward. Royler manages to secure a right hand grip on Megaton's right collar while his left hand controls the left sleeve.

2 Royler extends his right leg and puts his foot on Megaton's left thigh. He bends his left leg and drops his back to the ground, pulling Megaton down with him as if he wanted to pull guard.

1 DETAIL: Notice Royler's right hand grip on Megaton's right collar. All four fingers are inside and the thumb is outside.

3 When Royler's back hits the ground he pushes off his right foot and swings his body to his right so his head gets closer to Megaton's left foot and his body is almost 45° in relation to Megaton. Royler pushes off his right foot and pulls on Megaton's right arm to extend it and expose it for the arm-lock.

4 Royler drives his hips up and loops his left leg over Megaton's head, locking the calf on the back of his head while thrusting the hips up against Megaton's right elbow for the arm-lock. It is important to understand the dynamics of Royler's motion to better your chances of succeeding: Royler pushes off the right foot and pulls on Megaton's arm, helping swing his torso to the right. As he does this he loops the left leg around, using the momentum of his leg to help lift his hips and lock the leg over Megaton's head.

27. Shoulder-lock (omoplata) from standing

The shoulder-lock (or omoplata) from the standing grip fight is another one of Royler's options in his submission arsenal. Mastering a few of these submission options from the standing game will make you into a big submission threat which will open up other areas of the game. Your opponent's worry about being submitted will help you achieve take-downs more easily. Notice that the set-up for this submission is similar to the arm-lock. The differences are that your grip is on the outside collar instead of the inside one, and you will bait the opponent into thinking that you are simply pulling guard and change to the submission.

1 Royler and Megaton are fighting for grip control. They have a closed stance and their grips are similar: each holds the collar and opposite sleeve.

2 Royler places his right foot on Megaton's left thigh just above the knee and twists his torso to his right. He pulls down on Megaton's left collar with the right hand and up on Megaton's right arm with his left hand turning Megaton's torso to the left. Royler's hand motion is as if he was turning a big wheel.

3 Royler bends his left leg and drops to the mat while still pulling up on Megaton's right arm. Royler pushes off his right foot, driving his head and torso to his left so his body is almost at 90° with Megaton's right side. Royler continues to swing his torso to his left. He shoots the left leg up and around Megaton's right arm. Royler props up on his right elbow to help sit up.

4 Royler continues circling his left leg around Megaton's right arm and sits
up. Royler wraps his left arm around Megaton's back to prevent him
from somersaulting forward to escape the lock. Royler then brings both feet
around under his body in a circular motion as he drops his head towards the
ground. This motion gets his hips moving forward and forces Megaton's right
arm around the shoulder, torquing it for the submission.

28. Front clinch counter 1: Guillotine

The front clinch is a very common takedown attempt used in training and competition, especially by fighters with a wrestling background as they shoot for a single or double leg takedown. Every time your opponent attempts to use a front clinch he gives you the opportunity for a guillotine choke. The guillotine will work whether or not you are able to fend off the attack with a sprawl as Royler does here.

1 Royler and Megaton face each other. They are in an open stance with their hips facing out.

2 Megaton shoots forward for a clinch taking a deep step back with his right foot and wrapping his arms around Royler's legs. Royler counters the attempt by sprawling as he shoots his right leg back and bends the left to drive his hips forward and down. Royler places the right arm in front of Megaton's left shoulder to maintain distance and prevent Megaton from being able to lock his arms around Royler's legs. Royler is alert to the attack and, seeing the opening for the guillotine, he immediately wraps the right arm around Megaton's head.

3 Having defended Megaton's initial thrust, Royler raises his hips and head as he turns his torso to the left. Notice that Megaton is still fighting to secure control over Royler's legs. At this point Royler's right forearm should be locked right under Megaton's neck.

3 (REVERSE VIEW) Notice Royler's hand and body position. His hips are now pointing forward and slightly to the left; the torso is straight with the left arm back tight against his left side with the hand open ready to lock onto his own right wrist.

4 Royler locks the left hand (all five fingers together) around the bottom of the right wrist, locking the guillotine hold. He then cinches the grip around the neck so the head won't escape when he applies the guillotine. Royler steps forward, drives his hips forward and arches the body back as he pulls up on the right forearm with the left hand applying the chocking pressure on the neck. Notice that the guillotine choking pressure comes from the forearm moving up against the Adam's apple and not back towards Royler's body, as that would put pressure on the chin and not the neck.

4 DETAIL: Notice Royler's grip around Megaton's neck. The right forearm is wrapped tightly around the neck. The left hand cupping the right wrist will help pull it up and drive the forearm into the throat for the choke. Note that even if Megaton were successful at taking Royler down, the locked guillotine noose would still work. All Royler would have to do is pull guard as he falls down and apply the pressure to get the submission.

29. Front clinch counter 2: Head and arm triangle

At times there is so much commitment from your opponent's clinching attack that it may be hard to step forward and apply the guillotine. In that case the head and arm triangle works perfectly.

1 Royler and Megaton face each other. They are in an open stance with their hips facing out.

2 Megaton shoots forward for the front clinch. This time he drops his body very low and Royler is forced to sprawl even deeper so he shoots his right leg way back. Royler places the right arm in front of Megaton's left shoulder to maintain distance and prevent him from being able to lock his arms around Royler's legs. He wraps his right arm around Megaton's head and right arm with the hand showing up just under the right armpit.

3 Royler shoots both legs back out, bringing his hips down and dropping the weight of his body on Megaton's head, forcing him to the ground. At this point Royler locks the right hand over the biceps of his own left arm and places his left hand on Megaton's back to lock the head and arm triangle. Royler applies the submission pressure by bringing his elbows together and driving the right forearm up into Megaton's neck while at the same time pushing his chest down on Megaton's head, forcing it against the choking forearm.

3 **(REVERSE VIEW)** Notice how Royler sets up the head and arm triangle: the right forearm pushes in towards his left so the hand shows up under Megaton's right armpit. Royler extends the left arm and locks the right hand onto the left biceps. Royler presses his hips down to the ground using the weight on his body to press down on Megaton's head the entire time.

3 **DETAIL:** Notice how Royler applies the pressure. He bends his left arm so the left hand presses against Megaton's back. He brings his elbows together and presses his chest and head down against Megaton's head while driving the right forearm up and into Megaton's neck.

30. Front clinch counter 3: Head and arm triangle opponent succeeds

There are times when your reaction isn't quick enough to avoid the opponent's clinch. He will be able to secure control over your leg and will have the elements necessary to take you down. Even then you should be able to secure the head and arm triangle or the guillotine with a slight adjustment of the timing of the technique, as Royler demonstrates here.

1 Royler and Megaton face each other, each with an open stance.

2 Megaton shoots in with his right leg and is able to grab Royler's left leg with his right hand. Royler did not react quickly enough to sprawl and is forced to fight to avoid the takedown.

3 While he is fighting to stay standing Royler presses his chest down on Megaton's back and wraps his right arm around Megaton's neck, much in the same way as in the previous technique. As his right hand comes out under Megaton's right armpit, Royler grabs his own left biceps.

4 Royler then tightens his arm loop around Megaton's neck and right arm by bending the left arm and placing his palm on Megaton's back.

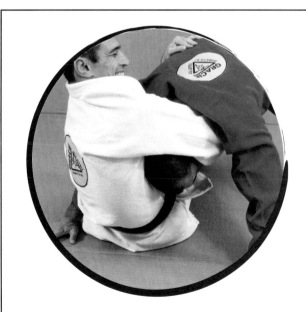

5 Royler then allows Megaton to take him down. He locks Megaton's right leg with his legs (wrapping the right leg around Megaton's right heel) for half-guard while pressing the choke by bringing the elbows together. He pushes the left hand down on Megaton's back so he can leverage the right arm up against Megaton's neck. It is important for Royler to trap Megaton's leg so he cannot jump or roll over Royler and take away the pressure of the choke.

5 (REVERSE DETAIL) Notice how Royler has his forearm under Megaton's neck. Royler's right elbow is on Megaton's left side so the forearm lines up just under Megaton's Adam's apple.

31. Takedown to reverse clock-choke

In the next three techniques Royler demonstrates a series of submissions when the opponent is on all fours. Having an opponent defend himself by turning to all fours is a very common situation during a Jiu-Jitsu match. He may turn to all fours to defend a guard pass, or simply get caught in that position during an exchange as in this case. The reverse clock-choke is especially effective from the takedown (in this case, a snapdown), as Royler demonstrates here, because your hand is already grabbing the opponent's collar, but the same attack works when you are on the ground on top of your opponent on all fours.

1 **Royler and Megaton are standing and fighting for grip control. They are both in a closed stance with similar grips, one hand on the collar and the other on the sleeves. In this case Royler's right hand holds Megaton's left collar.**

2 In a sudden jerking move Royler pulls Megaton forward and down with his hands and jumps to the left. Since Megaton is pressing forward against Royler's body, Royler's motion causes Megaton to lose his balance and fall forward. Royler is able to get to Megaton's side.

3 Royler's right hand remains on Megaton's right collar to set up the choke. Royler drops his chest on top of Megaton's back, preventing him from standing back up. Royler quickly switches his left hand from Megaton's right sleeve and grabs his left leg at the ankle instead.

4 Royler leans over towards Megaton's left side while still pressing on Megaton's back with his chest. He then drops his head down and summersaults over Megaton. When Royler's head hits the ground, he kicks his legs over, generating momentum to roll Megaton over as well. Royler pulls on Megaton's collar and left foot to help pull Megaton over. Royler ends up on his back with Megaton lying on top of him. Royler continues pulling Megaton's right collar with his right hand to choke him. Royler's left hand still holds Megaton's left leg.

5 Royler continues the rolling motion until he is on his knees on Megaton's left side. Royler presses his face down on Megaton's chest while his right hand pulls Megaton's collar, tightening the choke for the submission. Notice that Royler still holds Megaton's left leg to prevent him from rolling to his right to release the choking pressure.

32. Takedown to crucifix

It is common when using the previous takedown for the opponent to grab your leg with both arms as he hits the mats. This may happen because you did not move to the side quickly enough, and now your trapped leg makes it more difficult to go for the clock-choke variation shown above. In that case the crucifix is the perfect option to get a submission.

1 Royler and Megaton are standing fighting for grip control. Royler's right hand grabs Megaton's left collar.

2 As Royler attempts the takedown by pulling Megaton down to the ground with his arms, Megaton is able to grab Royler's right leg with his arms thus preventing Royler from executing the clock-choke.

3 Royler kicks his right leg back as he moves to his left breaking Megaton's grip around his right leg. Royler is now on Megaton's back. The pressure of his chest prevents Megaton from getting back up. Royler grabs Megaton's left ankle with his left hand while his right hand remains on Megaton's right collar. Megaton's right arm still holds Royler's right leg to prevent him from rolling forward and applying the clock-choke.

4 Royler switches his control and his hip position by
    bringing his left knee in towards his right knee. He
releases his grip on Megaton's left ankle, and slides the left
hand under Megaton's left armpit and holds the left wrist.
Royler then pushes off his left toes and lifts his hips and the
right leg to shift his weight onto his head and torso which are
pressing down on Megaton's left shoulder.

5 Royler extends the left leg, pushes off it and rolls over his left shoulder. Royler kicks the right leg over, bringing Megaton's right arm up with it, forcing Megaton to follow the roll or have to submit to an arm-lock. At the end of the roll Royler is on his back with Megaton lying on top of his chest. Royler's right hand pulls Megaton's right collar across for the choke while his legs trap Megaton's right arm to prevent him from rolling to his left to release the choke. Royler wraps his left arm around Megaton's left arm, sliding the left hand behind his head and forcing it forward, adding even more pressure to the choke.

33. Takedown to clock-choke

Royler here executes the same takedown as in the last two techniques. Megaton again is able to secure good control of Royler's right leg with his arms. This time Royler opts for the clock-choke instead of the crucifix because Megaton's grip is strong and prevents Royler from rolling over the shoulder. Royler switches his base and goes for the clock-choke.

1 Royler and Megaton are standing fighting for grip control. Royler's right hand grabs Megaton's left collar.

2 Royler steps back with his left leg, pushes off his right foot and pulls Megaton's torso down, forcing him to fall forward.

3 As he falls to the mat Megaton grabs Royler's right leg with both arms. Royler's right hand remains on Megaton's collar but since his hands are busy controlling Royler's legs Megaton does not defend the neck. Royler presses his chest down against Megaton's back and brings his left leg in towards the right.

4 Royler slides his left hand under Megaton's left armpit and grabs the left wrist.

5 Royler switches his hips so they face forward by sliding the left leg forward and kicking the right leg back, breaking Megaton's lock on his right leg. Royler applies the choking pressure with his right hand by pulling Megaton's collar up while his hips drive forward and puts his weight on Megaton's right shoulder, pressing it down. Notice how critical Royler's control on Megaton's left arm is. It prevents Megaton from rolling to his right to place his back on the ground and release the choking pressure on his neck.

34. Takedown counter: Choke

Winning a fight does not require that you always get the first move or even the second one before your opponent is ready to react. Many times your opponent takes the initiative and gets an attack on you. You need to be prepared for any eventuality and have a counter ready. In this case Megaton goes for a takedown and Royler counters it by taking the back and applying a choke.

1 **Royler and Megaton are standing facing each other with a standard grip of one hand in the collar and one hand grabbing the sleeve.**

2 **Megaton moves first. He steps in with his right foot in front of Royler's hips and tries for a hip throw. Royler counters it by driving his hips forward to take away Megaton's hip power.**

3 While Megaton still fights for the takedown by pulling Royler's right arm, Royler jumps up in the air and hooks his legs around Megaton's body above the waist.

4 Royler's left arm encircles Megaton's neck and his hand grabs over his own right bicep.

5 Royler bends the right arm back so the palm of his hand pushes the back of Megaton's head. Royler applies the rear naked choke by pressing the elbows in and tightening the "V" of the left arm around Megaton's neck while pulling the arms tight to press Megaton's neck.

5 DETAIL: Notice that to add extra power to the choke, Royler uses the left side of his head to press on his right hand, both forcing Megaton's head forward against the pressure of the arms.

35. Takedown to calf-cruncher

You don't need to wait for one move to be completed before you go on to the next. In fact, most of the time advanced fighters are already planning and setting up one or two moves ahead of the one they are executing. In this case Royler goes for a leg trip takedown as he prepares the calf-cruncher.

1 Royler and Megaton are standing facing each other with a standard grip of one hand in the collar and one hand grabbing the sleeve. Royler leans back and pulls Megaton with him.

2 When Megaton reacts by pulling back Royler quickly steps forward and circles his right leg around Megaton's right leg to trap it. At the same time Royler bends his knees to drop his body down slightly and reaches with his right arm between Megaton's body and right arm so his forearm is over Megaton's right thigh and the hand touches his own (Royler's) right calf. Notice that Royler still has a grip on Megaton's right sleeve with his left hand and his right shoulder pushes against Megaton's right bicep.

3 Royler uses his right shoulder to push Megaton's arm back while his entire body weight pushes forward and down on Megaton, forcing him to fall to the mat. Royler plants his left hand wide to control his fall and uses it to hold his torso off the ground. Royler kicks the left leg over so he can roll forward over the right shoulder.

4 As he rolls forward Royler bends the right leg in and loops the left leg over the right foot locking the figure-4 around Megaton's right thigh. Royler reaches with his hands and pulls Megaton's right foot back, forcing the calf against his shin bone for the submission.

4 DETAIL: For best results and to inflict the most pain, Royler makes sure to have the forward blade of his right shin bone pressed against Megaton's calf.

36. Takedown counter: Arm-lock

Royler demonstrates a very clever and effective counter to the leg sweep takedown. Notice that Royler wastes no time even when he is seemingly on the losing end of a positional battle. Even as he is falling he is already setting up the submission.

1 Royler and Megaton are standing facing each other with a standard grip of one hand in the collar and one hand grabbing the sleeve. Megaton leans back and pulls Royler with him.

2 Royler's reaction is to lean back to regain his balance. Megaton takes advantage of this to apply the takedown. Megaton moves forward and swings the right leg past Royler's right leg. He kicks it back, hooking it on Royler's right leg on the way back for the trip. At the same time Megaton pulls Royler's right arm with his left hand and pushes Royler's left shoulder with his right arm, forcing Royler's torso to spin and adding to the takedown.

2 DETAIL: Even as he is falling Royler prepares the submission. While he is starting to fall he points the right knee in and slides the shin in front of Megaton's hips.

3 Royler doesn't let go off his grip on Megaton's gi as he falls to his right. He pulls Megaton down with him. When Royler's back hits the ground his right shin is in front of Megaton's hips and his left leg is already looping over the head. Royler locks the left leg over the left side of Megaton's head.

4 Royler extends his body by thrusting his hips up and against Megaton's right elbow for the arm-lock.

37. Standing guard passing attack: Loop choke

Whenever you are fighting, opportunities for submission appear all the time. Frequently, when you attack your opponent he gets distracted defending the submission attempt which allows you to advance your position. In this case Royler is standing trying to pass David's guard. David is focused on using the sitting guard to prevent Royler from reaching his objective. Royler sees David's distraction and uses the loop choke to catch him.

1 Royler is standing and attempts to pass David's guard. Royler's right hand grabs David's right collar and his right leg is forward. David defends by sitting up and wrapping Royler's right leg with his arms.

2 Royler drives the right knee into David's chest to keep him back as he drops the right elbow down slightly so his forearm hooks under David's chin. Royler reaches with the left hand behind David's head.

3 Royler pulls David's head down with the left hand and loops the right arm around David's neck.

4 Royler bends down and reaches with the left hand to grab under David's right ankle.

5 Royler ducks his head between David's torso and right leg so he can roll forward over his right shoulder.

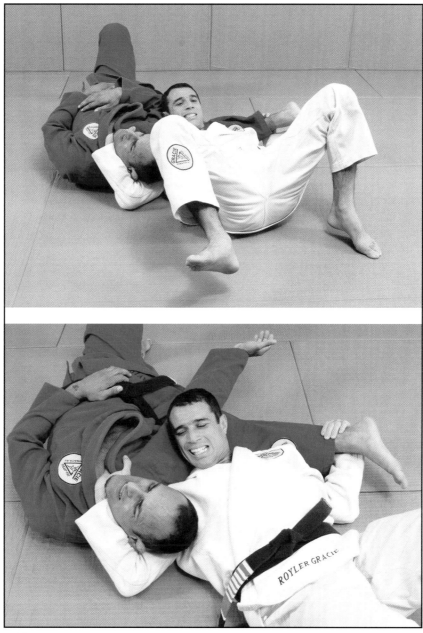

6 Royler ends up with his back on the ground. His right hand pulls David's collar tight against his throat while his left hand controls David's right ankle so he can't roll to his left and release the pressure of the choke. Notice that Royler's head presses on top of David's right arm and torso. Royler pushes off his head to raise his chest adding leverage and tightening the choke.

38. Standing guard passing attack: Arm-lock

Often times your opponent will turn to all fours (turtle) as an attempt to defend your guard pass. In this case Royler is standing and reaches Megaton's side as Megaton turtles to defend the completion of the pass.

1 Megaton is in the turtle position. Royler grabs Megaton's belt with his left hand and pushes down to pin Megaton's hips in place. Royler's right hand grabs Megaton's collar near the back of the neck pressing it down as well.

2 Royler steps forward with his right leg, hooking the foot over Megaton's right thigh near the hips.

3 While maintaining pressure on Megaton's back and hips Royler steps out with the left foot and spins his body 180° so his feet point back where he started. Notice that Royler's right foot and toes now hooks under Megaton's right thigh.

4 Royler switches his grip and is now using the right hand to grab Megaton's belt. Notice that Royler grabs under the belt with the palm facing up. Royler's left hand reaches between his legs and grabs Megaton's right sleeve near the elbow.

5 Royler sits down and rocks back. As he rocks he pulls Megaton's belt up with the right hand and kicks the right foot up, raising Megaton's right leg and forcing him to roll over. As Megaton's legs reach vertical Royler's back is on the mat. At this point he spins his torso to his left as he pulls Megaton's right arm over his hips. Royler loops the left leg over Megaton's face. When Megaton completes the forward roll and his back and legs reach the ground Royler has completed the arm-lock and raises his hips to apply pressure to the elbow joint for the submission.

39. Standing guard passing attack: Triangle

Another great option for attacking the sitting guard when standing is to go for the triangle. Royler is a great study of his dad's techniques and there are many similarities in their pref-erences. In many situations Royler uses a variation of the Grandmaster's attack (technique 10) but goes for the triangle instead of the arm-lock.

1 **Royler stands in front of David trying to pass his guard. David is using the sitting guard with his right hand controlling Royler's collar. David's left hand is on the ground with the arm posted back, helping him move his hips to follow Royler and block his path to his side. Royler grabs David's left gi sleeve at the wrist with his right hand and under the elbow with his left hand.**

2 **Royler leans back, pushing off his feet and pulling David's right arm with him. This extends David's right arm and exposes it.**

3 David reacts by pulling his arm back and bending it at the elbow. Royler follows the pull and steps over David's left shoulder with his right leg. Royler locks the knee just over David's left shoulder, presses his calf on David's back and presses his hips up on David's right arm.

4 Royler bends his left leg and does a controlled fall forward on his right leg which is now bent under David's back. He plants his right hand on the mat to use the right arm as a brace and turns his body to his right. Royler pushes David's right arm to his left and locks the right foot over the left leg for the triangle (figure-4) around David's right arm and head. Royler squares his body with David's and applies the choking pressure by pulling David's head up with his hands while squeezing the knees together.

40. Side control attack: Leg-lock

Side control is one of the most stable positions in Gracie Jiu-Jitsu. Because of its stability it is an extremely good position to launch submissions. One such submission is the leg-lock demonstrated here by Royler. This attack takes advantage of the opponent's defensive leg position, as he will lift his near leg to block any mount attempts on your part.

1 Royler has side control on David's right side. Royler's left elbow is tight against the left side of David's face to keep his head from moving. His right hand touches the mat next to David's right hip to prevent him from bringing the right leg in to replace the guard.

2 Royler pushes off his hands and lifts his torso up while sliding the left knee over David's stomach. At the same time Royler wraps his right arm around David's right leg under the knee and pulls up on the leg.

3 Royler pivots around David's right leg by spinning his body to his right and bringing the right leg forward so his thighs and knees frame David's right leg. At the same time Royler wraps both arms around David's leg and drops his back to the mat as he pulls David's ankle back. Royler applies the pressure on the knee for the leg-lock by raising his hips and pushing them against the knee while pulling David's ankle back towards the ground. Note that it is important for Royler to have his knees tightly pressing together against David's leg to secure the position and also to have his left knee up so the shin keeps David from rolling up to his right and on top of Royler to defend the leg-lock.

41. Side control attack: Shoulder-lock

This is one of Royler's favorite and most lethal submissions. The shoulder-lock from side control is both sneaky and effective. Your opponent will not be expecting the arm lock, and won't be aware of what is really coming until it is too late. The key to this attack is the pressure on the chest and the arm wrap.

1 Royler has side control on David. He is on David's right side and has both elbows on the left side touching the mat. David has good defensive posture with his left hand under Royler's right armpit.

2 Royler starts the set-up by wrapping the left arm under and around David's left arm. Royler makes sure his arm wraps above David's elbow to trap it. If he doesn't control the elbow, David would be able to escape easily by sliding his arm from Royler's grip. Royler places the left hand on his own right shoulder while at the same time he pushes his right arm against David's left forearm.

3 Royler starts stepping to his left, making sure to keep his chest pressing down on David's chest. As he moves Royler grabs his own left elbow with his right hand. Rolyer brings his elbows in towards each other to press David's arm.

4 When he reaches the north-south position, Royler brings his knees in so he can raise his chest slightly while still maintaining pressure on David's chest with his belly. He adjusts the position by locking David's arm tightly. He does so by placing his left hand on his right bicep and pulling the left elbow with his right hand.

4 DETAIL: Check out Royler's lock on David's arm: his chest presses against David's arm, the left bicep pushes against David's tricep and the left hand holds his own right bicep. Royler's right arm frames David's arm as it presses under the forearm with the right hand holding his own left elbow.

5 Royler turns his shoulders counter-clockwise and switches his hip position so they face towards David's feet. He brings his right leg under the left and shoots the right foot forward. Royler turns his shoulders to torque David's arm around the shoulder for the submission.

42. Side control attack: Toe-hold

The toe-hold from side control is another attack that takes advantage of your opponent's defensive posture in blocking the mount. The keys to this attack are the surprise element and the quick application of the submission once the hold is set. If you apply pressure slowly you will allow your opponent to defend the hold and perhaps escape. If you use this attack, once you start, you have to go for it. Apply the pressure quickly and without hesitation and you will submit your opponent.

1 Royler has side control on David's right side. His left elbow is next to David's left ear and his right hand is next to the right hip. David has good defensive posture with his right foot resting on the left knee so his leg blocks Royler from mounting him from the side.

2 David's left foot is exposed, and Royler sees the opening for the toe-hold. He slides his right arm between David's legs and readies his hands for the attack with the fingers together and the palms facing down.

3 Royler grabs the top of David's right foot over the toes with the left hand and locks his right hand onto his left wrist, forming a figure-4 around David's foot. As soon as he locks the hold, Royler applies the pressure by pulling David's toes in towards his chest, torquing the foot around the ankle for the submission.

3 DETAIL: Notice Royler's figure-4 hold on David's foot. His left hand holds the instep by hooking the outside edge of the foot with the fingers. Royler's right hand locks onto his left wrist with the forearm pushing just under David's Achilles. Royler pulls the toes towards his chest in a counter-clockwise motion, torquing the foot around the ankle.

43. Side control attack: Lapel Choke

The side control lapel choke is Royler's trademark. He probably has submitted more people with it than just about any other choke. This is a subtle and solid choke that when mastered will yield many submissions.

1 Royler has side control on David's right side. Royler's left arm is wrapped under David's head with the shoulder pressing against David's chin to keep the head from turning.

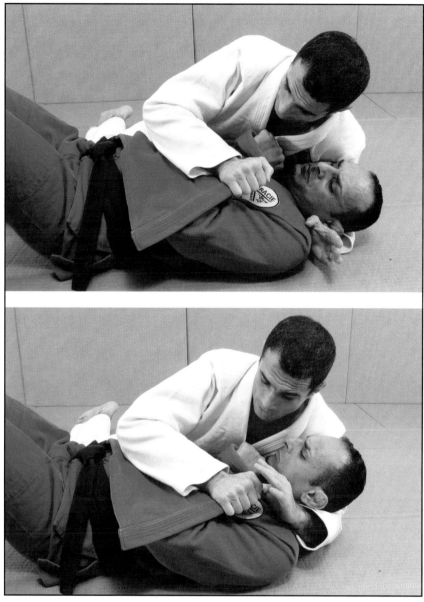

2 Royler turns his shoulders and hips clockwise. With his right hand Royler grabs David's right lapel, loops it over David's left arm and tries to deliver it to his left hand. David defends it by using his left hand to grab the collar and push it out.

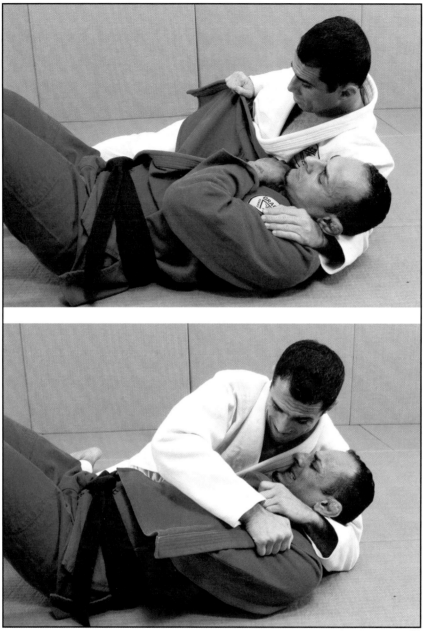

3 Royler turns the shoulders again, slides the hand down the collar slightly and repeats the move, looping the lapel again and securing it tightly with his left hand. Notice that David's left hand is now trapped and pressing up against his own throat.

4 Royler slides his right arm under David's left arm, making sure his arm presses tightly against David's arm to lift it up.

5 Royler twists his hips back so they face towards David's head by switching his leg position. He slides the right leg under and loops the left one over. Royler tightens the choke by pulling David's collar with the left hand while at the same time Royler curls his right arm up. This lifts David's left arm up and drives the left fist into David's own throat.

Note: This choke will work even if the opponent doesn't grab the collar to defend, and is even easier to apply with the same mechanics because you do not have to subdue the opponent's resisting arm.

44. Side control to knee-on-the-stomach attack: Parallel choke

The parallel choke from the knee on the stomach is a very powerful choke that will surprise many an opponent. Normally the choking hand comes in grabbing the opposite collar in a crossing pattern. In this case the first hand does not change position from the normal control (behind the neck) so it doesn't alert the opponent to the impending submission.

1 Royler has side control on David's right side. His left hand is wrapped under David's head gripping the back of the collar and his right hand grabs David's belt in preparation to going for the knee on the stomach.

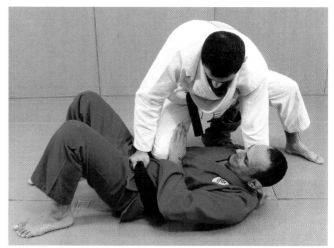

2 Royler pushes off with his arms and springs his body up. He slides the right knee over David's stomach as he steps out with the left leg for the classic knee-on-the-stomach position. David reacts normally, defending the knee on the stomach by pushing Royler's right knee with his left hand.

3 As David worries about escaping the knee on the stomach Royler slides his right hand with the palm facing up, (the fingers in and the thumb out) and grabs David's left collar as close as possible to his right hand grip.

4 Royler steps to his left and brings his elbows and forearms together. The right forearm presses down against David's throat while the left one pushes David's head up for the choke.

4 DETAIL: Notice Royler's grip and forearm position for the choke: his left hand grabs as close to the right hand as possible with both thumbs pointing in the same direction. The forearms push together with the right forearm coming down and the left coming up.

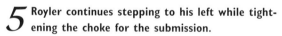

5 Royler continues stepping to his left while tightening the choke for the submission.

45. Side control to knee-on-the-stomach attack: Choke

Royler here takes advantage of another common reaction to the knee on the stomach. In this case David attempts to stop Royler from reaching the knee on the stomach by grabbing Royler's collar and pulling it down. When this happens Royler immediately goes for the choke.

1 Royler has side control on David's right side. His left hand is wrapped under David's head gripping the back of the collar and his right hand grabs David's belt in preparation to going for the knee on the stomach.

2 Royler pushes off with his arms and springs his body up. He slides the right knee over David's stomach as he steps out with the left leg for the classic knee-on-the-stomach position. David reacts by grabbing Royler's collar and pulling him down with his left hand.

3 Royler drops his torso back down slightly without taking the right knee from David's stomach. He traps David's left arm by wrapping his right arm around the elbow and grabs his own collar with the right hand.

4 Royler steps over David's head with his left foot, trapping David's head between his left foot and left hand. He chokes David by raising his chest up and driving his left arm forward, pushing against David's neck. At the same time Royler presses the left calf down for the submission.

46. Side control attack: Own lapel choke (near)

Royler likes to vary his attacks. He believes that if you have a wide variety of submission options you will make your job easier as your opponent will always be off-guard guessing what might be coming next. This choke is another one of his sneaky chokes from his lapel choke arsenal. The key to this choke is that Royler uses his own collar in a very non-threatening way.

1 Royler has side control on David's right side. His left arm is wrapped under David's head with the shoulder pressing against the chin. Royler reaches back with his right hand and holds his own left lapel (near David's head).

2 Royler lifts his torso up slightly so he can pass the lapel in front of David's torso to reach his left hand.

3 Royler's right hand gives the lapel to the left hand. Notice that Royler grabs the lapel about six inches up from the end and pulls it down against David's throat.

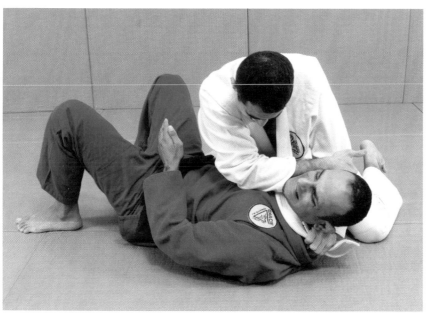

4 Royler raises his torso up and slides the right arm along the right side of David's face. He can either slide the right hand along the left sleeve or grab the left sleeve to add pressure to the choke. At the same time he pulls his own lapel with the left hand, tightening it around David's neck for the choke.

47. Side control attack: Own lapel choke (near): Variation

A very strong variation of the previous choke is shown here. Both chokes are effective, however this one is especially powerful, as you will really tighten the collar when you spin to the other side of the opponent.

1 Royler has side-control on David's right side. His left arm wraps under David's head with the shoulder pressing against the chin. Royler reaches back with his right hand and holds his left lapel.

2 Royler lifts his torso up slightly so he can pass the lapel in front of David's torso. Royler's right hand gives the lapel to the left hand. Notice that Royler grabs the lapel about six inches up from the end and pulls it down against David's throat.

3 Royler plants the right hand on the mat near David's right side and steps out with the right foot as he raises his torso.

4 Royler continues to move to his left. When he is at 180° with David's body he extends the legs back and drops his head to the mat. Pushing off his feet and hand and pivoting off his head Royler lifts his legs up and jumps over David, ending up on his left side. Notice that this move caused Royler's collar to tighten up around David's neck.

4 (REVERSE VIEW) Check out Royler's stance before he jumps over. The top of his head is on the mat next to David's side, Royler's right hand is on the mat near his head and the right foot is planted out right and the left foot planted to the left.

5 Royler grabs David's collar with his right hand and chokes him by bringing his elbows together and pulling the collar tight with both hands.

5 DETAIL: Notice how Royler grabs David's collar behind his head with the right hand and brings his elbows together. The left elbow moves down and the right one moves up to press against the sides of David's neck, choking him.

48. Side control attack: Arm crusher

This is a devastating and extremely painful submission from side control. Royler starts as if he is going for a kimura. When the opponent resists and defends by grabbing his own belt he switches to the arm crusher.

1 Royler has side control on David's right side and secures the kimura lock on David's left arm.

1 DETAIL: Royler's right hand grabs David's left wrist while his left arm is wrapped around David's left arm. Royler's left hand grabs his own right wrist, securing the kimura figure-4 lock on David's left arm. David counters the attack by grabbing his own belt with his left hand.

2 Royler steps over David's head with his left foot and pulls on David's left arm, turning David's body to the right as if he was still fighting for the kimura.

3 Realizing that David has a strong grip and will not easily yield the kimura, Royler changes to the arm crusher by stepping over David's body with his right leg and sitting down on David's chest. Royler drops his body to the mat, pulling David with him, and bends and wraps his right leg around David's left arm.

4 Royler locks the left leg over his right foot as if he were doing a triangle on David's left arm and applies the submission pressure by bringing his knees together, forcing David's arm to press in against Royler's forearm. The pressure on his arm makes David feel as if his arm is going to explode!

4 (REVERSE VIEW) Check out how Royler twists his left arm so the forearm has its widest part between David's arm near the elbow. By having the wide part of the arm instead of the flat part between David's arm, Royler adds more pressure to the submission.

49. Side control attack: Wrist-lock

The wrist-lock is a very versatile submission. Once you realize how to apply it and the elements required for it to work you will see opportunities to use it from various posi- tions and situations. In this case Royler notices David's exposed left hand pressing against his shoulder and immedi- ately goes for the wrist-lock.

1 Royler has side-control on David's right side. He has both arms on David's left side. David's left hand pushes against Royler's left shoulder so he can drive the forearm against Royler's neck to create space.

2 Royler sees that David's hand is vul- nerable to the wrist-lock and goes for it. Royler wants to lock David's hand in place so he cannot remove it and escape the attack. He uses his left hand to push David's left forearm in while at the same time he cups his right hand behind David's left elbow and drives his chest down, pressing against David's hand.

3 Royler cups both hands behind David's elbow and pulls it up and against his chest while at the same time he drives his chest forward and down, pushing David's hand backwards for the wrist-lock.

3 DETAIL: See how Royler cups the left hand over his right. Both push up against David's elbow to force the wrist while at the same time Royler drives his chest forward and down for the submission. Royler pulls David's elbow up, forcing the wrist even more.

50. Side control attack: Americana

In order to be a good fighter, you need to be able to link techniques in a sequence you can vary depending on your opponent's counters until you catch him. Here, Royler first tries the wrist-lock as in the previous position, but as an option, or if the wrist-lock is not available, he goes for this attack. This is a very clever use of the Americana submission. Royler takes advantage of David's near arm position to trap it and uses his hips to apply the pressure for the submission.

1 Royler has side control on David's right side. His left arm is on the left side of David's head and his right arm blocks David's right hip. David's his left arm pushes against Royler's left shoulder and his right arm presses against Royler's hips.

2 Royler grabs David's right elbow with his right hand and switches his hips so they face towards David's feet by sliding the left leg under the right one until his left hip touches the mat. Royler's right arm traps David's right arm with the hand cupping David's elbow and the armpit and elbow pressing on David's hand and forearm.

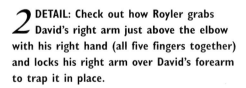

2 DETAIL: Check out how Royler grabs David's right arm just above the elbow with his right hand (all five fingers together) and locks his right arm over David's forearm to trap it in place.

3 Royler loops his left leg over David's legs.

4 Royler pushes off his left leg and raises his hips up as he arches his torso back and to the right. This motion causes his armpit to push David's right wrist down for the Americana. The pressure for the submission is in the rotation of the arm around the shoulder, torquing the joint.

51. Side control bottom attack: Reverse arm-bar

Generally when your opponent has side-control on you, your thoughts should be directed towards defense first and escaping the position second. Your opponent has reached your side and he is looking either to advance his position and mount you or to use one of the many submissions available from side-control. There are not too many submissions available for the person on the bottom, however at times you may find the opportunity to use this reverse arm-bar and surprise your opponent for a submission.

1 David has side-control on Royler's right side. He has his left arm wrapped around the bottom of Royler's head but his right arm ends up between Royler's legs. This is generally a mistake and Royler takes advantage of it.

2 Royler grabs David's right sleeve with his left hand so he cannot readjust his arm position and then wraps his right arm around David's left arm.

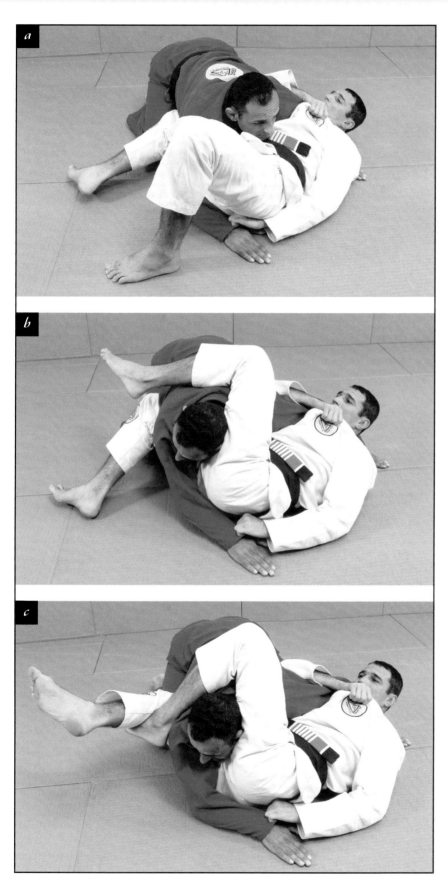

3 Royler pushes off his left foot and escapes his hips to his left, turning his body to the right at the same time. Royler loops his left leg over David's head and locks the right leg over the left foot locking David in a reverse triangle with his right arm and head trapped in Royler's figure-4.

4 Having trapped David in the triangle, Royler reaches up with his left hand and grabs David's left sleeve near the wrist. Notice that Royler kept his right arm wrapped around David's left arm throughout this entire movement.

5 Royler pulls David's left hand from under his head and locks his left wrist onto his own right wrist, securing the figure-4 lock on David's right arm. Royler drives David's left wrist up with his right hand while he drives his right forearm down, pushing David's left elbow down and hyperextending it for the reverse arm-bar submission.

5 (REVERSE VIEW) Check out how Royler applies the pressure on David's right elbow by pushing the left hand up and pressing the elbow down with his forearm.

52. Side control attack: Collar and leg choke

Like father, like son. This is one of Grandmaster Helio's favorite chokes from side-control. It also happens to be one of Royler's favorite submissions. As he points out: "My father is always fond of chokes and he taught me this one as well as many others. I saw him use this one a lot so I decided to prac- tice it until I got it down!" The secret to this choke is that the choking pressure comes from three sources: your arm pulls the collar around the neck while at the same time your forearm and calf press against the opponent's neck.

1 Royler has side control on David's right side. Royler's left arm is wrapped under David's neck and his right arm hooks around David's left elbow. Royler grabs the back of David's collar directly under his head with the left hand.

2 Royler shifts his hips so they face towards David's head; he slides the right leg forward and loops the left leg back, planting the foot on the mat. Royler turns David to the right by pulling David's left elbow with his right arm. Notice that by turning David to the right Royler tightens the collar on the right side of the neck. Royler pulls David's head up with the left arm. Note: Royler keeps the left arm perfectly straight so the blade of his forearm presses against David's neck.

3 Royler loops his left leg over David's head.

4 Royler plants his left foot on the mat next to David's head and locks the back of his leg on top of David's face. Royler applies the choking pressure by pulling the collar with his left hand while the forearm presses against the right side of David's neck. At the same time Royler continues pulling up on David's left elbow, turning him to the right and pressing his left calf against the left side of David's neck.

53. Side control attack: Spine-lock

This is a vicious and effective submission from side-control. It is not a commonly used position which makes it even more effective. Royler takes advantage of the opponent's reaction of raising his right leg to get him in a spine-lock. Notice that from the side control with the hips up, Royler can either go for an Americana lock on David's right arm or for this option.

1 Royler has side-control on David's right side. Royler has both elbows on the mat on David's left side. David's right forearm blocks Royler's left hip and his left arm is tucked under Royler's right armpit.

2 Royler grabs David's right elbow with his left hand. He shifts his hips to face David's head by pushing off the left foot and sliding the right leg under the left. Royler's right arm wraps around the back of David's neck. Royler ends up with the right leg flat on the ground parallel to David's body. Royler's left leg is bent slightly so he can push off the foot to apply pressure with his weight on David's chest.

3 Royler wraps the left arm under David's right leg and pulls it up. Notice that Royler makes sure he hooks the crease of the arm under David's knee for optimum leverage.

4 Royler raises his left leg off the ground until he can hook his left hand under his thigh close to the knee.

5 Royler begins to apply pressure on David's spine by putting his left leg down and bringing his knees together. Royler stretches his legs out and pulls David's head towards his legs intensifying the pressure on the spine for the submission.

54. Side control attack: Brabo choke

A great choke from many positions is the brabo choke. The brabo choke uses the opponent's lapel not only to choke but also to control his movements, making it a very controlling attack. Once you have achieved control of the lapel, the choke is almost finished. From there it is simply a matter of patience: wait for the opponent to expose the arm or the other collar for the finish.

1 Royler has side control on David's right side. David's left arm is tucked under Royler's chest and the right arm is hidden under Royler's right armpit. Royler's left arm is wrapped around David's neck. Royler pulls open David's left lapel with his right hand.

2 Royler extends his legs and pushes off his feet to lift his hips off the ground, adding his weight to the pressure on David's chest. Royler feeds the collar to his left hand making sure to pass it under David's left arm. At this point David's collar presses against his left armpit and controls both his torso and head movement.

3 Royler springs up and slides his right knee onto David's stomach. At the same time Royler pulls David's collar tight with his left hand so it comes out on David's right side of the head where he can grab it with his right hand. Notice that Royler grabs the collar with his four fingers in and the thumb on the outside.

4 David attempts to defend the knee on the stomach by pushing against Royler's right knee with his hands. Royler grabs David's left sleeve and pulls the arm up and across his body with his left hand.

5 Royler continues to drive David's left arm all the way across the body so that it presses against the left side of David's neck. Royler drops his right shoulder down to apply his body weight on David's left arm and press it against the neck. At the same time he pulls up on David's collar with his right hand, pressing the right side of the neck with his right forearm and choking David.

5 DETAIL: Look how Royler's right forearm presses the side of David's neck and David's left arm presses the opposite side for the choke. Also notice how Royler uses his chest to press against David's left arm to add pressure to the choke.

55. Side control attack: Multiple attacks to key-lock (Americana)

At the highest levels of competition, one has to constantly feign different attacks and connect many attacks together in order to be successful. In this case Royler sets up a position with many attacks and feints one to get the other.

1 Royler has side control on David's right side. Royler's left hand is near David's head while his right arm is under David's left arm.

2 Royler wraps his right arm around David's left arm. Royler extends the left leg out and pushes off it to raise his hips off the ground while at the same time he grabs under David's right elbow with his left hand and pulls the arm up.

3 Royler slides the right leg under the left one until his hips are switched and facing towards David's head. Royler has his right hand pressing against his own right ear, locking David's arm in place. From this position Royler has several attack options: he can attack either of David's arms for an arm-lock.

4 David senses the attack on his left arm and tries to defend it by bending the arm, sliding it over Royler's head and bringing the hand towards his own head.

5 In one movement Royler quickly reaches and grabs David's left wrist with his left hand and locks his right hand onto his own left wrist as he slides the right leg back under the left to turn his hips down. Royler continues turning his hips towards David's feet as he pushes David's wrist around in a clockwise direction with his left hand to torque the arm around the shoulder joint for the submission.

5 DETAIL: See out how Royler uses the right side of his face together with his arms and hands to control David's arm. By pressing the side of his face against David's left arm while his right arm presses the arm in the opposite direction Royler is able to secure control over David's arm and prevent him from pulling the elbow out of the lock.

56. Side control attack: Multiple attacks to key-lock near arm

Royler demonstrates yet another attack from the same controlling position: a key-lock on the near arm.

1 Royler is in side control on David's right side. Royler controls David's arms while switching the hips as in the previous technique. This time David worries about his right arm and bends it back to free it from Royler's control.

2 Royler catches David's right wrist with his left hand and guides it down between his legs.

3 Before he releases his grip on David's wrist, Royler bends the right leg and locks it over David's left forearm.

4 Royler loops and locks the left leg over his right foot. Notice that Royler makes sure to have David's arm above the elbow resting on his thigh while the forearm is under his calf.

5 Royler pushes off his left foot and extends his body as he drives his left knee back and thrusts his hips up to force David's arm to twist around the shoulder for the key-lock.

57. Side control attack: Multiple attacks to head and arm choke

Having multiple attack options from any position is always good. The side control position offers a variety of submission possibilities. Learn and try as many as you can and in the end you will naturally select a few to become part of your well-oiled arsenal. Royler demonstrates another option from the side control. David tries to use his forearm to push Royler's head away and Royler exploits the opening and goes for the head and arm choke.

1 Royler has side control on David's right side. His right arm is in front of David's left arm and the left arm hooks under David's head controlling the head. In an effort to create space David puts his left forearm under Royler's throat and pushes up.

2 Royler gives in to the push and arches his torso back.

3 Royler deflects the power of David's forearm by hitting the elbow with his right hand and driving it towards David's head. Royler pushes his head against David's triceps to lock David's left arm in place. Royler clasps his hands together. At this point Royler has David's head and left arm trapped between his head and arms.

4 While still keeping pressure on David's head and arm, Royler leans forward with his torso and pushes off his feet, jumping over David's body and landing on his left side.

5 Royler extends his legs and pushes off the tip of his toes. He drives his body against David's left arm while pulling his arms together. Royler's head pushes David's left arm against the left side of his neck while Royler's left arm presses the opposite side of the neck for the choke.

58. Side control attack: Choke to arm-lock (Double attack)

In this technique Royler shows a choke from the side control and then, upon a successful defensive counter, a sequence to the arm-lock. This choke from side-control is very effective and the defense counters can lead to many attack opportu- nities such as this arm-lock or a key-lock on the outside arm. Be aware of the options and switch back and forth between them as the opportunities arise.

1 Royler has side control on David's right side. Royler's right hand touches the mat next to David's right hip to prevent him from sliding the right knee in and try to replace the guard. Royler's left arm is on the mat such that the elbow is next to the left side of David's face which prevents David from moving his head and therefore his body. David's right arm is under Royler's chest with the hand on his back while his left arm is under Royler's chest near the head with the hand under the left armpit.

2 Royler lassoes David's right arm with his right arm and reaches with his hand until he can grab David's collar just to the right side of his head.

2 **(REVERSE VIEW)** Royler lassoes David's right arm. He makes sure to wrap above the elbow, otherwise David can easily pull the arm out.

2 **DETAIL:** Notice how Royler grabs David's collar: the palm faces up, and the fingers are wrapped over the collar to grip the inside of the collar while the thumb remains on the outside. Royler grabs the collar just to the right of David's head.

3 Royler attempts the choke. He wants to grab David's left collar with the left hand, thumb in and fingers out, and slide the elbow down towards the mat next to David's right ear. This forces the bottom blade of the forearm against David throat to choke him. David blocks Royler's hand and arm from securing the choke by extending his left arm slightly forcing Royler's chest away

4 Royler and David fight for the attack and the counter. Royler switches to his next option: the arm-lock. He slides his knees next to David's body and raises his torso. This extends David's right arm which had been trapped by Royler's right arm. Royler plants the left hand on the mat next to David's left ear.

5 Royler pushes with off his left hand and springs to his feet. His left leg loops around David's head with the heel touching down next to his hand. Royler's right knee slides over the top of David's right ribcage. Notice that Royler retains control over David's right arm during this entire movement.

6 Royler drops his body to the mat, his legs pressed against David's right arm. Royler's right armpit traps David's wrist and as he arches back drives the arm back with it. Royler raises his hips, pressing them against David's elbow and hyper-extending it for the arm-lock.

5 & 6 (REVERSE VIEW) Notice how Royler locks his right elbow next to his side and against his thigh, completely trapping David's arm, while at the same time he slides his right knee over David's right ribcage. When Royler drops to the mat, his armpit locks David's wrist and forces the arm back while his hips press the elbow up.

59. Mounted attack: Single lapel choke

Many times when you mount an opponent he will try to escape using the "shrimping" or elbow escape method by turning to one side, coiling his leg and trapping one of your legs. This choke is particularly effective for that situation, but the same choke can be used from the back or half-guard (with minor adjustments) as well.

1 **Royler is mounted on David. He grabs David's right collar with his right hand to set up a choke. David prepares the elbow escape by dropping his left leg to the mat and bending the right leg to plant the right foot on the mat.**

2 **David pushes off his right foot, slides his right arm under Royler's right arm and turns to the left as he tries to shrimp his body and trap Royler's right leg between his legs. Royler plants the left hand on the mat for balance and switches to the side-mount by sliding the left knee up towards David's head, raising the right knee up and tucking the right foot up against David's stomach to prevent David from trapping that leg. Royler pulls David's collar open with his right hand and reaches around David's head with his left arm.**

3 Royler's right hand feeds the collar to his left hand. Notice how Royler's left hand grabs the collar with the left thumb in, the fingers on the outside and the wrist slightly bent so it fits tightly against the curvature of the neck.

4 Royler pulls David's gi pants on the outside of the right knee with his right hand and starts to lean back. Notice that at this point Royler's right foot is off the mat and the calf presses down on David's side.

5 Royler continues to lean back while pulling on David's right leg with the right hand and pulling on David's collar with his left hand to tighten the choke. Royler loops his left leg over David's left arm, trapping it with the foot. Royler continues leaning back and pulls his torso to the right with his right hand pulling on David's right leg while at the same time pulling David's collar with his left hand. This adds tremendous pressure to the choke.

60. Mounted attacks: Collar choke (Double attack 1)

Another great attack option from the mount when the opponent tries to elbow escape is this collar choke. Again Royler quickly reacts to David's escape attempt by going to the side-mount and applying this choke. This time however David's right arm stays over Royler's right arm as he tries the elbow escape.

1 Royler is mounted on David. Royler grabs David's right collar with his right hand to set up a choke. David prepares the elbow escape by dropping his left leg to the mat and bending the right leg to plant the right foot on the mat.

2 David pushes off with his right foot, slides his right arm over Royler's right arm and turns to the left as he tries to "shrimp" his body and trap Royler's right leg between his legs. Royler plants the left hand on the mat for balance and switches to the side-mount by sliding the left knee up towards David's head, raising the right knee up and tucking the right foot up against David's stomach to prevent David from trapping that leg. Royler still maintains his right hand grip on David's collar.

3 Royler's right hand feeds the collar to his left hand. He grabs the collar with the thumb in and the fingers out. Once he has secured the grip on the collar, Royler slides his right hand, with the arm looped under David's right arm, behind David's head. Notice that Royler's right hand has all the fingers together and the palm facing towards his chest. Also note that Royler's arm remains wrapped around David's right arm.

4 Royler extends his body up by pushing off his right foot and left knee. He applies the choke by pulling David's collar with his left hand while sliding the right forearm behind David's head to push the head forward against the collar. Notice that Royler makes a fist with his right hand, sliding it over his left forearm and directing it down as if he wanted to punch the mat. Royler extends his arms as if he wants his fists to touch each other.

61. Mounted attacks: Collar choke (Double attack 2)

At times when applying the previous choke, the opponent may try to defend the choke by blocking the right arm from coming through; you should switch then to the arm-lock. Notice that this and the previous technique are also interchangeable and can be used in conjunction in what is commonly called a "double attack". The technique starts in similar fashion when you use either submission, giving the opponent two attacks to worry about.

1 Royler mounts on David. His right hand grips David's right collar at the ear, palm up. David turns to his right as he tries to escape. Royler switches to the side-mount and feeds David's right collar to his left hand.

2 David blocks Royler's attempt to slide the right arm behind David's head by locking his right arm over Royler's arm.

3 Royler switches to the arm-lock. He grabs his own left collar with his right hand.

4 Royler plants the left hand on the mat directly in front of David's face to block his head from moving. He swings the left leg back around by pivoting on the knee so his toes touch the mat and the leg lines up with his body. Royler drops his chest down on top of David's right arm to prevent him from yanking the elbow out to defend the arm-lock. Pushing off his right foot and left hand, Royler swings his left leg over David's head and drops his body to the mat, extending his torso and taking David's right arm with him. When his back hits the mat, Royler pushes off his heels and thrusts his hips up against David's elbow while pulling the wrist down with his hands, hyperextending the elbow.

62. Mounted attack: Triangle

Whenever you mount your opponent you need to be aware of his escape options so you can take advantage of his reactions to get a submission. There are two ways to escape the mounted position: the upa (also called the bridge) and the elbow escape (or shrimping). In the previous techniques

Royler demonstrated a few options when the opponent options for the elbow escape. Here he shows a solid option when the opponent tries the upa – going for the triangle choke.

1 Royler is mounted on David and has his right hand inside the right collar to set up a possible choke. David loops his left leg over Royler's right leg, trapping it with his foot in preparation of an upa escape.

2 When David bridges up Royler escapes his right foot and opens the leg out. He plants it wide to his right while at the same time bracing his left hand on the mat to stop David's bridge.

3 David hooks his left arm under Royler's right leg and tries to slide his body under it to do a back-door escape and escape through Royler's legs. Royler pivots on his right foot, dropping the knee in and to his left.

4 Pivoting off his left arm, Royler slides the left knee up towards David's head, bends the right leg and brings his right foot in. Royler reaches around David's head with his left arm, grabs his right ankle with his left hand and swings the left leg forward to extend it. Royler leans to his right to help the right leg come under David's head.

5 Royler leans forward with his body while still holding his right ankle with his left hand until he can lock the left leg over his right foot, locking the figure-4 around David's right arm and head.

6 Royler applies the triangle choke by bringing his knees together, thrusting the hips forward and pulling David's head up with his hands.

63. Mounted attack: Arm-lock

Good things happen when you achieve the mounted position and begin to attack. Your opponent now has at least two things to worry about: escaping the mount and defending the attack. By incorporating more than one option in your attack combinations you add difficulty to his recognition and increase his reaction time, thereby increasing your changes of success. In this case Royler starts with a choke and switches to the arm-lock when David correctly counters the choke.

1 **Royler is mounted on David. His right hand grabs David's right collar to set up a choke. David grabs Royler's right forearm with both hands and pulls it to his chest to defend the neck and prepare for an upa escape.**

2 **Royler grabs David's left sleeve with his left hand.**

3 Royler steps forward with his right foot so the leg hooks under David's left arm and slides his hips up and to his left while leaning to his right with his torso. Royler's left knee slides up to the right side of David's head. The leg is open with the toes pressing against the mat, ready to react.

4 Royler swings the left leg over David's head and falls to the mat as the heel hits the ground.

5 Royler drops his torso to the mat, extending David's right arm as he falls. Royler hooks his right arm under David's right leg to prevent him from pushing off it to escape the attack and thrusts his hips up against David's right elbow to hyperextend the joint.

64. Mounted attacks: Nutcracker choke

The nutcracker choke is a very quick, effective and surprising choke when properly applied. The keys to this choke are the surprise element and your commitment to the choke. If you execute it half-heartedly it won't work, so when you decide to go for it, apply 100% pressure and get the finish.

1 Royler is mounted on David. David grabs both of his own collars with his hands to defend the collar choke. Royler grabs David's collars with his hands, but contrary to the normal choke grip the fingers are in and the thumbs are on the outside pointing down.

2 In one move, Royler drops his chest down towards David's chest and presses his knuckles in against David's neck. At the same time he grapevines his legs on David's leg to prevent him from bridging to escape. Notice that in this case Royler's elbows are open with the arms pushing the knuckles against David's throat for the choke.

2 DETAIL A: Royler rolls his hands down to force the knuckles to press against the side of the neck. Royler maintains the grip on the collar to add extra leverage to the choke.

2 DETAIL B: Royler hooks his feet on David's shins making it harder for David to free up the legs and attempt an escape.

65. Mounted attacks: Sleeve choke

Another highly effective attack from the mounted position is the sleeve choke. This is a powerful and sneaky choke, and the key again is to set it up so you don't alert the opponent to your intentions.

1 Royler is mounted on David with his hands on the ground for balance. David's elbows and arms are close to his body and neck to defend a regular collar choke.

2 Royler wraps his left arm around the back of David's neck. He does so in a calm non-threatening manner so David does not senses the imminent danger. Royler then grabs the inside of his right sleeve with his left hand. Notice that Royler inserts all four fingers on the inside of the sleeve and the thumb on the outside with the palm of the hand pointing down. Royler's right hand is open with all five fingers together in a blade.

3 Pivoting over the sleeve, Royler swings his right hand over David's head and slips the bottom of the hand on top of David's Adam's apple.

4 Royler slides his hips to the left and the left knee up towards David's head as he raises the right knee off the mat. Royler applies the choke by extending his arms. As he extends the arms the left forearm pushes David's head up while the right hand slides down the left forearm to press against the Adam's apple for the choke.

66. Mounted attacks: Arm-lock variation

Often times when you achieve the mount your opponent will quickly and desperately try to scramble to escape, especially if he isn't an expert in ground fighting. Even advanced fighters commit mistakes in their haste to escape a difficult position such as the mount. In this case David commits one of the cardinal sins when mounted: he extends his arms to push Royler off him, allowing Royler to catch him with this arm-lock variation. Note: Do not underestimate your opponent's scrambling ability, even if he is a total beginner. The force of his efforts may surprise you and result in you losing the position so be ready for his scramble, especially the stiff arm push. First maintain your position and then focus on submitting your opponent.

1 Royler is mounted on David. David extends his arms and tries to use his hands to push Royler's chest away and escape the mount. Royler knows that he needs to maintain position first so he deflects David's push with his left arm by leaning forward and to his left, planting the left hand on the mat for balance, while turning his shoulders to his left to deflect the power of the push.

2 Royler shoots the right hand inside David's left arm until his elbow is past David's arm. He uses the forearm to deflect David's left arm away. Royler uses his left arm as a pivot and balance point as he leans further to his left to help wrap his right arm around David's arm.

3 Royler continues wrapping his right arm around David's left arm and traps it against his chest. Royler steps forward with the right leg and points the knee in to lock the thigh just under David's left tricep and fully locking David's arm in place. Notice that Royler's right armpit helps to trap David's forearm.

4 Royler leans over and turns his body to his left by pivoting off his left hand and knee. Royler's thigh under the tricep forces David to turn to his own right. Once David is on his side Royler can easily slide the right knee over David's head until it reaches the ground. Notice that Royler keeps his right foot hooked on David's head to control his movement and ability to escape. Royler applies the arm-lock pressure by arching his torso back while driving his hips down and applying pressure to the elbow joint.

4 DETAIL: Notice how Royler's knees are both pressing against David's arm to take away any space for him to pull his arm out. Also notice Royler's pelvis pushes forward against David's elbow while his right armpit drives David's forearm back for the arm-lock.

67. Mounted attacks: Knee split

Royler doesn't care how he finishes his opponents. Royler likes to say, just as his father does: "I take whatever they give me!" This leg split from the mount is both vicious and surprising and is a great way to finish a fight.

1 Royler is mounted on David. David keeps his elbows tight against his body with the hands protecting his neck. He hooks Royler's right foot with his left foot in preparation for an upa (or bridge) escape. Royler grabs David's collars near his stomach and pulls them open.

2 Royler leans forward, dropping his weight on David's chest, and underhooks David's neck with his left arm to counter the upa. He then wraps David's left collar under David's left arm with his right hand and feeds it to his left hand.

3 Royler reaches back and grabs David's left knee with his right hand.

4 Royler leans back slightly as he pulls David's left leg out with his right hand and foot causing the leg to pivot around the knee joint for a painful submission. Notice Royler controls David's torso with the arm wrapped around the head and the hand pulling the collar that is wrapped under David's armpit to prevent him from escaping the lock.

68. Back attacks: Collar choke

Having someone's back is the best possible position you can have in a Gracie Jiu-Jitsu match or a street fight. With your opponent unable to see what your arms and hands are doing, you have a great advantage in the battle for control and submission: you can anticipate his movement, and he will not be able to anticipate and effectively counter yours. In this case

Royler demonstrates one of the best and most basic yet effective chokes from the back. Notice that the word "basic" does not mean antiquated or ineffective in Gracie Jiu-Jitsu. Actually, it means just the opposite. Basic situations occur frequently, so basic techniques will be used often, and, when properly mastered, they yield great results.

1 Royler has David's back with both hooks on (Royler's heels and calves dig on top of David's thighs to control his ability to move and escape the back control). Royler's left arm is wrapped under David's left arm and the hand controls David's left collar pulling it down taut.

2 Royler wraps the right arm around David's neck. He places the right thumb inside the left collar and slides the hand up, using it as a guide to reach as high a grip on the collar as possible.

3 Royler wraps his fingers around the collar to secure the grip while folding the collar over towards his left.

3 DETAIL: VERY IMPORTANT: Notice that Royler doesn't simply grab the collar flat but rather folds it over, making a much better handle to grip and also creating a blade against David's neck. This is an extremely important and an often overlooked detail that will make your chokes much more effective and also improve your ability to remain in control of the grip on the collar. If you do not fold the collar over it may slip out from between your fingers as you tighten the choke.

4 Royler bends the left arm at the elbow so he can reach around the back of David's head. The bottom edge of Royler's hand faces towards the back of David's neck.

5 Royler extends his body by pushing off his legs. He pulls the collar across and up with his right hand while extending his left arm so the bottom blade of his hand pushes down on David's neck and forces the head forward for the choke. Notice that for maximum pressure Royler's arm and shoulder motion is as if he wanted to straighten both his arms and turn his shoulders slightly to his left.

69. Back attacks: Collar choke to arm-lock

Your opponent is not a static dummy and will try to defend most attacks that you attempt. Although you have a timing advantage when you have back control, he will still try to defend and counter your choke attempts. In this case Royler starts with the previous choke, but when faced with a good defense on David's part, he switches to the arm-lock to catch David. Notice that the key to this attack combination, like most other attack combos, is to maintain the pressure and the commitment to the first attack until the last second, when you quickly switch to the second option. Otherwise your opponent will sense the change and start counter measures for your second attacking option.

1 Royler has back control on David and begins to attack the collar for the choke.

2 As Royler reaches with his right hand to grab the left collar, David intercepts the attack by grabbing Royler's right wrist with his right hand making it difficult for Royler to secure the proper grip. Royler can fight David's counter and try to improve his grip.

3 Royler turns his body to his left as he tries to slide the back of his left hand around David's head. David further defends the choke by closing the left arm to prevent Royler from advancing his left arm. Royler can fight David's counter and try to improve his grip until he can choke him or he can simply opt for the arm-lock.

4 Sensing that he doesn't have a good
enough grip for the choke, Royler switches
to the arm-lock. He releases his right hook from
David's thigh, allowing him to spin his body
until it is perpendicular to David's. Notice that
Royler is still pulling on David's collar to both
distract him and apply choking pressure while
driving the head down to the ground.

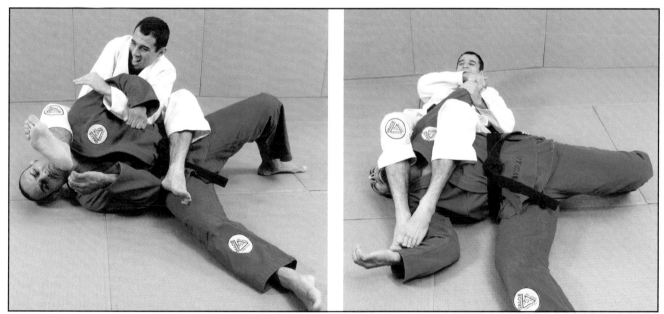

5 Royler quickly releases his grip on the collar and loops the right leg over
David's head to press it down with the calf. Notice that Royler's left arm
remains wrapped around David's left arm in perfect control for the arm-lock.
Royler extends his body as he grabs David's left wrist with both hands and
pulls it against his chest, extending the arm. Royler presses his calves down
while driving his hips up against the elbow for the arm-lock.

70. Back attack: Opponent stands up: Arm-lock

Regardless of how much control you attempt to have over an opponent, sometimes in the dynamics of the match things happen so that he is able to escape your control. In this specific case David is able to stand up and use a wrestler's escape of bracing on all fours and tries to pull Royler down to the ground. This is a very common escape to the back control

and Royler has just the right attack for these situations. Preparation and recognition are very important elements for effectively submitting your opponent. Notice that Royler is always looking for the opening to submit his opponent and is always preparing the attack as the positions develop and has at least one attack option ready.

1 Royler has back control with hooks on. David has a good defensive position with his elbows in tight and his hands protecting his collar.

2 David turns to his right and begins to roll to his knees. Royler first makes sure to maintain back control. He uses his left hand to grab David's left shoulder so he can follow David's roll, otherwise David may be able to spin and keep Royler on the ground and end up on top in Royler's guard.

3 David gets to his knees and Royler remains on his back with his hooks on.

4 David pushes off his hands and gets up while maintaining a four-point base
with his feet and his palms on the ground. This is a critical position here as
David can grab Royler's head or gi and pull him down and to the side until he
gets him to the mat, escaping the position. It is very hard for Royler to avoid
David's defense even with his hooks in because of the angle of David's legs, arms
and torso. Royler puts his palms on the ground to brace himself and delay David's
escape.

5 Anticipating the possibility that he may be pulled down and lose the position
Royler begins his attack. While still bracing off his left arm Royler wraps his
right arm around the inside of David's right arm as he slides his body down
David's arm and to the right side pointing the right knee in (Royler slides down
David's arm as if he was sliding down a pole). As Royler is sliding down his torso,
David thinks that he is escaping the position and doesn't sense the danger of the
imminent attack.

6 Royler continues sliding and turning his body to the right until his right
shoulder hits the ground. He releases the left foot hook from David's hips and
swings the leg back. Royler exchanges the control by sliding the right foot over
David's left thigh and hooking it there. Notice that Royler has David's right arm
fully in control with his armpit trapping the wrist and the right arm trapping
David's arm.

7 Royler loops the left leg over David's head, locking it under the chin, and
extends his body by driving the hips forward against David's elbow for the
arm-lock.

71. Back attack: Opponent stands up: Triangle

Royler demonstrates another great attack option for the same escape as he goes for the triangle instead of the arm-lock. Royler may execute this attack simply as a matter of personal choice because he prefers the triangle over the arm-lock or because David countered the attack by bending his right arm, thereby making it more difficult for Royler to execute the arm-lock.

1 David attempts to escape Royler's back control by rolling and standing on his hands and feet in a four point stance.

2 While still bracing off his left arm, Royler wraps his right arm around the inside of David's right arm as he slides his body to the right side. This time, however, he keeps the left foot hooked inside David's leg and slides the right leg in front of David's hips.

3 Royler grabs his right ankle with his left hand and pulls the leg in between David's arms and towards his own chest.

4 Royler releases the left foot hook from David's leg and lets his body fall to the mat. He pulls his right leg tight around David's head as he swings the left leg back. Remember that David's right arm is trapped by Royler's right arm.

5 Royler locks his left leg over his right foot, completing the figure-4 lock around David's right arm and head for the triangle choke. Royler brings his knees together while at the same time pulling David's head down with both hands to apply the choking pressure.

72. Back attack: Opponent bridges: Triangle and arm-lock

One of the most effective ways to escape the back control is to bridge and turn to one side until you can get your shoulders on the ground. If his opponent attempts this move, Royler immediately opts for this countering attack which takes advantage of the opponent's bridge.

1 Royler has back control with hooks on David. Royler has both arms under David's arms with the hands gripping the collar for extra control. David attempts to escape by bridging.

2 Royler releases his hooks and loops both legs around David's legs, hooking the feet under the thighs. He then extends his legs, kicking David's legs up, and uses the weight of their legs to help him rock forward and sit up. Royler ends up sitting behind David with his legs out.

3 Royler loops the right leg over his own and David's right arms and reaches with his left hand to grab his right ankle.

4 Royler pulls his right ankle tight towards his chest, locking David's left arm and head.

5 Royler then loops his left leg over the right foot and locks it in place for the figure-4 triangle lock. Royler can apply the triangle choke from here.

6 Royler turns his body to his right, bracing off his right elbow, and wraps the left arm around the inside of David's left arm. Royler makes sure to lock the wrist with his armpit.

6 (REVERSE VIEW): Notice how Royler drives his elbow around David's arm so he can lock the wrist with his armpit.

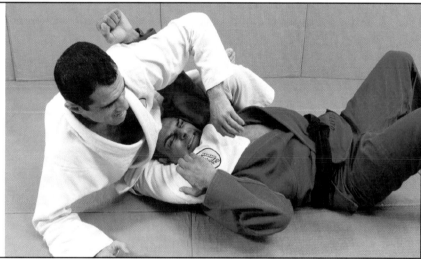

7 Royler leans back and extends his body to drive his hips up against David's elbow as his back pushes David's wrist down for the arm-lock.

73. Turtle position attack: Banana split

Often the opponent turns to all fours or the turtle position to defend the guard pass or to escape side control. Attacking the turtle presents its own sets of difficulties and opportunities. As the opponent closes himself up to prevent you from placing your hooks and take his back, he also exposes himself to submissions such as the clock choke, the crucifix and to being turned over. In this case Royler uses a vicious submission called the "banana split".

1 David is in the turtle position with Royler on his back controlling the left arm with his left hand. David uses his right hand to grab his own collar to prevent Royler from grabbing it and applying a clock choke. Since his right arm is tied up defending the choke David cannot block a roll to that side.

1 (REVERSE VIEW) Watch how Royler slides his right foot in front of David's right thigh and hooks his foot over the ankle for the first hook. At the same time Royler keeps the right arm and the left leg open to maintain his balance and remain on top of David.

2 Royler locks his right hand onto his left hand and pulls the arm up, making sure his left forearm presses against David's left shoulder. At the same time he leans his body to his right which forces David to roll over.

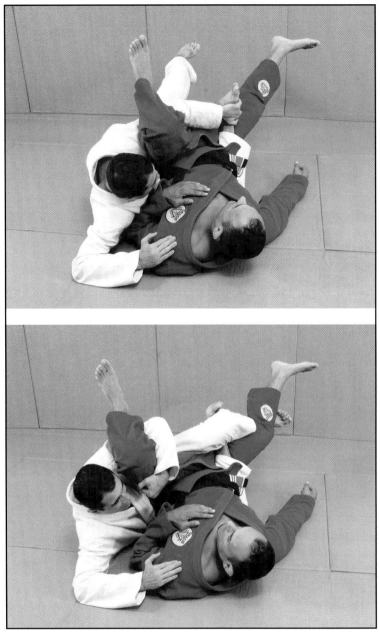

3 Royler sits up slightly and pulls his right foot with his left hand. He loops the left leg over the right foot and hooks the left foot behind David's knee setting the figure-4 around David's right leg. Royler then wraps David's left leg with his left arm.

4 Royler locks the right hand with the left and pulls the left arm back, forcing the forearm on David's thigh. He extends his body using the arms to pull the left leg to open while using his legs to push David's right leg in the opposite direction for the "banana split" submission.

4 DETAIL: Notice how Royler turns his left arm so the blade of the forearm presses against David's thigh to add pressure to the leg.

74. Turtle position attack: Calf-lock

Royler shows another great option from the turtle roll here as he chooses to go for the calf-lock instead of the banana split. Both positions are equally effective; it is just a matter of personal preference as to which one you are going to use.

1 David is in the turtle and Royler uses the same method as in the previous technique to roll him over: hooking the right foot onto David's right leg, clasping his hands together and pulling the arm up against David's left arm near the shoulder.

2 When David's back hits the ground Royler props himself up with his right
arm and sits up. Royler hooks the right foot behind David's right calf.

3 Royler pulls David's right foot towards himself, making
sure that his shin bone lines up behind David's calf.

4 Royler loops his left leg over the right foot and locks it
in place. He then drops to the ground while still pulling
David's foot towards his chest. At the same time Royler
extends his body, forcing his shin against David's calf for
excruciating pain and a submission.

4 DETAIL: Notice how the blade of Royler's
shinbone is positioned to press directly
on David's calf. It is very important for Royler
to have David's leg as close to his own
(Royler's) ankle as possible as that area has
the least padding around the shinbone, which
makes it even more painful for David when
Royler applies the pressure.

75. Half-guard attack: Choke

This is another of Royler's sneaky attacks. When Royler has one hand on the collar and the other arm is propped back, the opponent is not worried about a choke. When Royler sneaks in the second hand to grab the belt instead of the collar, the opponent is still not thinking choke, until it is too late and he realizes that he is defeated. Although Royler demonstrates this choke from the half-guard it can work from the closed guard as well.

1 **Royler has David in his half-guard with his legs trapping David's right leg. Royler's right hand grabs David's right collar and his left arm is propped back so he can sit up.**

1 **DETAIL: Check out Royler's grip: the right hand grabs the collar with the fingers in and the thumb on the outside. Royler's wrist is bent and the top blade of the right forearm presses against David's throat. Notice that whenever Royler raises the right elbow he applies pressure on David's throat with the forearm.**

2 Royler sits up further as he reaches over the left side of David's head with his left hand and grabs David's belt.

3 Royler leans back and chokes David by pressing the left elbow down against David's shoulder while he raises the right elbow up, forcing the forearm against David's throat for the choke.

3 (REVERSE VIEW) Royler applies the pressure by pulling David's right collar with his right hand and raising the right elbow up while at the same time he pulls David's belt with the left hand and forces his left elbow down against the back of David's left shoulder.

76. Half-guard attack: Brabo choke

As we pointed out before, the brabo choke can be used from various positions. Previously Royler used it from side-control but he can also use the same choke from the mount, the guard and even the half-guard (bottom or top) as he demonstrates here.

1 Royler is in David's half-guard with his right leg trapped between David's legs. Royler grabs David's left collar under the arm and passes it to his left hand.

2 Royler extends his right leg and pushes off the foot as he raises his hips and torso while pulling David's collar tight with his left hand. Seeing the space that Royler gives him, David turns to his right as he tries to escape and replace the guard. That is exactly what Royler wants.

3 Royler pulls the collar, slides the right arm in front of the right side of David's neck and grabs David's collar with his right hand.

4 David tries to release the choking pressure on his neck by reaching with his left hand and pulling Royler's arm. Royler takes advantage of David's defense by grabbing David's left sleeve with his left hand and pulling the arm across his body so it presses against the left side of David's neck.

5 Royler turns his hips to the left as he drops the right shoulder down, pressing on David's left arm with his chest. At the same time Royler pulls up on David's collar with his right hand to choke David.

5 DETAIL: Notice how Royler uses his left hand to grab the edge of David's sleeve and drive the arm across the body. Royler's right forearm presses David's neck on the right while David's own left arm presses the left side of the neck for the choke. Also notice how important it was for Royler to allow David to turn to his right. This let Royler tighten the collar half of the choke while giving him the perfect angle to use his bodyweight against David's arm for the choke.

77. Half-guard: Kimura and the counter

One of the most common attacks when you are in the half-guard top is for the opponent to attempt a kimura on your outside arm. This is a very solid and dangerous attack that should not be taken lightly. Whenever you are faced with a submission attempt from your opponent remember it is always best to defend it first and only after the defense

counter with a submission. In this case however Royler's defense is also a counter submission as he turns the tables around and applies a kimura back to the attacker David. Notice that this position demonstrates two submissions, the kimura from the half-guard bottom and the counter for the person on top.

1 Royler is in David's half-guard with his right leg trapped between David's legs. Royler has his left arm open and posted on the ground for balance. David decides to attack that arm with a kimura. David grabs Royler's left wrist with his right hand to prevent Royler from pulling the arm away as he prepares the attack.

2 David rolls over to his right and loops the left arm around Royler's left arm above the elbow. David grabs his right wrist with his left hand to secure the figure-4 lock around Royler's right arm. David is ready to apply the kimura on Royler's right arm/shoulder. David wants to twist Royler's right arm in a counterclockwise direction around the shoulder.

4 Royler arches his torso back and thrusts his hips forward
   to push the left forearm and elbow up. This forces
David's left arm to pivot around the shoulder for a kimura.

3 Royler realizes he is in a dangerous situation so his first
   thoughts are to defend the danger. Royler pushes off his
right hand, blocking David's hip so he cannot follow Royler,
and raises his torso. He bends the left arm in until he can
grab his right arm with the left hand. At this point David no
longer can execute the kimura as Royler's arm right forearm
acts as a block stopping the left one from pivoting. Notice
however that Royler's counter actually created a figure-4
around David's left arm.

78. Guard attack: Break the posture to choke

This is a very clever choke. Generally the opponent senses danger when the hands of the attacker grab opposite sides of the collar. In this case Royler grabs one side of the collar with both hands to give Megaton a false sense of security; Megaton won't recognize the threat until it is too late to counter.

1 Megaton is in Royler's closed guard. Royler grabs the right side of Megaton's collar with both hands. The left hand, with the palm facing down (fingers on the outside and thumb on the inside of the collar), grabs near the right side of the neck while the right hand is palm up (fingers on the inside and thumb on the outside) and grabs the collar near Megaton's chest. Royler has to leave enough space between his hands to clear over Megaton's head.

2 Royler pulls the collar to the left side making sure his left elbow stays wide, forcing Megaton to lean to that side as well. At that point Royler loops the left arm over Megaton's head.

3 Royler loops the left arm over Megaton's head, ending up with the regular collar choke position with the forearms pressing on the sides of Megaton's neck.

3 DETAIL: Royler applies the choking pressure by wringing the hands so the knuckles point up and by pulling the arms back so the elbows reach towards the ground and tighten the collar.

79. Guard attack: Break the posture to arm-bar 1

Often times when faced with a good guard the opponent tries to stall and secure his posture before attempting to pass the guard. In this case Megaton has both hands on Royler's lapel with the arms bent and the elbows down close to Royler's hips. This is a very common defensive position that can be used for stalling. It is also a difficult position to break down especially if you are pressed for time and need to attack (as in the end of a match that you are losing on points). Royler not only shows here a solid way to break the control but also continues to an arm-bar submission.

1 Megaton is in Royler's guard. He holds Royler's lapel with each hand with the arms bent and the elbows near Royler's hips for a good defensive posture.

2 Royler wants to break down Megaton's control and posture. He unlocks his legs, places both feet on the ground and pushes off them, thrusting his hips up and bridging. As he reaches the top of the bridge Royler circles his arms under Megaton's arms. He leads with his hands inside Megaton's forearms to break Megaton's control.

3 As he drops his hips back down, Royler turns his body to his left and places the left hand on top of Megaton's right biceps, blocking it in place. He wraps his right arm around Megaton's left arm until he can reach Megaton's right collar with the right hand. Royler places his right foot on Megaton's left hip and pushes off it to extend his body and escape his hips to his right. At this point Royler's arm is wrapped around Megaton's left arm directly over the elbow and Royler's armpit traps Megaton's wrist.

3 DETAIL: Notice how Royler uses his left hand to grab and open Megaton's right collar making it easy for the right hand to come in (fingers inside and thumb on the outside) and secure a good grip. This is a very useful detail when you want to wrap your opponent's arm and grab his collar or simply grab the collar. Use one hand to help the other secure the grip.

Royler puts his left foot on Megaton's right hip and pushes off it to help further turn his body to his left (counterclockwise) as he presses his right leg against Megaton's left side.

4 Royler continues turning to his left and pressing the right knee down against Megaton's left side while at the same time he arches his torso back. Royler's back drives Megaton's wrist back while his right arm (and especially his right elbow) presses down on Megaton's left elbow for the arm-bar.

80. Guard attack: Break the posture to arm-bar 2

Another great way to break your opponent's base and posture is to wait for his move and take advantage of the openings it offers. In passing the guard, the opponent first has to break open your closed guard. To do so he generally needs to move to a more upright position and some practitioners choose to stand up altogether. Look for his movement as he starts to shift his weight to stand up or raise his hips and take advantage of it. In this case Royler uses a similar idea as in the previous position and ends up with another arm-bar submission.

1 Megaton is in Royler's guard. He has his hands on Royler's chest and readies himself to push off them to stand up. Royler waits for the right moment to make his move.

2 Megaton leans forward as he tries to adjust his weight and stand up. As soon as he senses Megaton's weight shift, Royler loops his arms around Megaton's arms by bringing his hands inside while opening his legs and kicking them up towards his head. Note that Royler's legs still press in against Megaton's side. Royler's arms break Megaton's base and his leg movement forces Megaton to fall forward.

3 Royler's left arm grapevines around Megaton's right arm, circling it at the elbow. Royler uses the right arm to hold Megaton slightly away so he can have enough room to maneuver his body.

4 Royler places his right hand on Megaton's arm near the shoulder and locks his left hand over his right wrist, firmly securing a figure-4 grip on Megaton's right arm while his armpit traps Megaton's wrist. Notice that Royler's arms are close to his chest for maximum leverage.

5 Royler puts the left foot on Megaton's right hip and pushes off it, raising his hips up, and locks the right leg over Megaton's back with the calf pushing down to prevent him from pulling away. Royler's rising hips apply pressure to Megaton's elbow for the arm-bar.

5 DETAIL: Notice how Royler's right calf prevents Megaton from pulling away from the arm-bar. Also check out Royler's hand position: the right hand is on top of Megaton's right arm near the shoulder. Royler has the figure-4 around Megaton's arm with the left forearm pressing the elbow.

81. Guard attack: Break the posture to triangle

Breaking the opponent's posture is one of the keys to succeeding not only in defending the guard but also in attacking and submitting him. Royler here uses the same motion to break Megaton's posture but this time demonstrates a different and clever way to reach the triangle choke.

1 Megaton is in Royler's closed guard. He has good posture and his hands are grabbing Royler's gi at the chest. Megaton's elbows are held close to his torso.

2 Royler opens his legs and pushes off his feet to bridge his hips up while circling the arms inside Megaton's arms to break Megaton's grip and posture, forcing him to fall forward.

3 Megaton uses his hands and arms to brace his fall. Royler immediately takes advantage of Megaton's open arms. He escapes the hips to the right and turns his shoulders to his left, then wraps his right arm around Megaton's left arm and uses the left hand to keep Megaton's right arm open.

4 Royler places his right foot on Megaton's left hip and pushes off it to adjust his distance so he can coil and bring the left leg in and place the left foot on Megaton's right bicep. Royler uses his left hand to push Megaton's wrist out so the arm is open to make it easier for his foot to come in.

5 Royler loops the right leg over Megaton's back until he can hook the right foot under the right arm. Notice that Royler has to move and adjust his body in order for his foot to reach and hook Megaton's arm. He does so by using the left foot to push Megaton's arm open; he uses the same push on the arm to help move his hips out to the right.

5 DETAIL: Royler's right foot under Megaton's arm will keep Megaton's arm open and allow Royler to release the left foot from the bicep for the triangle. Without the right foot hook, Megaton would be free to use his arm and bring it back to safety between Royler's legs when the left foot is released from his bicep.

6 Royler slides the left leg over Megaton's right shoulder.

7 Royler locks the right leg over the left foot for the triangle figure-4 around the head and left arm and pulls Megaton's left arm across his body over to the left.

8 Royler applies the triangle choke by pressing his knees in while pulling Megaton's head down with both hands.

82. Guard attack: Break the posture to brabo choke

Royler demonstrates another great way to break the opponent's posture and immediately follow it with a choke. In this
case Royler uses the grip on Megaton's lapel to assist in
breaking the posture.

1 Megaton is in Royler's guard with good posture.
Both hands grab Royler's gi near the chest, his
arms are slightly bent and his elbows are close to
his body. Royler counters by grabbing Megaton's
lapels near the chest, the left arm over and right
arm under Megaton's arms.

2 When Megaton shifts his weight forward to try
to get up, Royler opens his legs and pulls the
collar towards him, forcing Megaton to fall forward.
Megaton opens his arms and plants the hands on
the ground to prevent him from hitting his head on
the mat.

3 Royler slides the right hand down Megaton's collar so he has enough room to loop it under Megaton's armpit and around the back of the head, and hands the collar over to his left hand.

4 Royler pulls Megaton's collar out with his left hand. He then reaches with his right hand on the right side of Megaton's neck and grabs the collar. The first grip in the choke is always very important, even more so in the brabo, so Royler's first grip (the right hand) should be very tight against Megaton's neck.

CLOSE UP: While still pulling the collar with the left hand so it is taut, Royler slides the right hand along the collar to get a solid grip as far behind Megaton's head as possible.

4 DETAIL: Notice how Royler curls the left hand so his knuckles point towards him, making it easy for his right hand to grab the outside edge of the collar.

5 Royler releases his left hand's hold on the collar and grabs the left side of Megaton's gi over the shoulder. The grip is with the palm facing down and the fingers grabbing the top of the cloth. Alternatively, Royler can grab the same lapel (left lapel) near Megaton's left shoulder. Royler pulls Megaton's head close to his chest with his arms, elbows aiming towards the ground, and applies the pressure for the choke.

83. Guard attack: Break the posture to brabo choke variation 1

This time as Royler attempts the brabo choke, Megaton blocks Royler's left hand from grabbing the collar in an effort to defend the attack. Royler then switches to this variation of the choke.

1 Megaton is in Royler's guard with good posture. Both hands grab Royler's gi near the chest, his arms are slightly bent and his elbows are close to his body. Royler counters by grabbing Megaton's lapels near the chest and pulls Megaton forward as he tries to shift his weight.

2 Royler uses the right hand to feed the collar to the left hand in the same manner as in the previous technique. Royler ends up with Megaton's left collar wrapped under the left arm and around the back of the neck with the left hand pulling it away from the neck. Royler then uses his right hand to grab the collar at Megaton's neck.

3 Royler wants to grab Megaton's gi on the left shoulder to finish the choke but Megaton intercepts and blocks Royler's hand from reaching the collar with his own left hand.

4 With his left hand Royler grabs Megaton's left sleeve and pulls the arm across his chest while turning his own torso to the right. Notice that by pulling Megaton's arm across Royler actually uses the arm as it presses on the left side of his neck to choke Megaton, while Royler's right arm presses the right side of the neck.

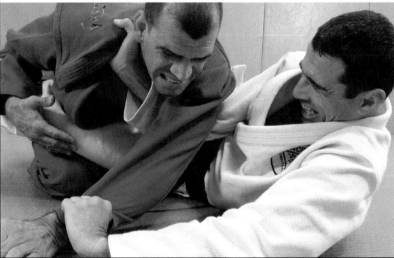

84. Guard attack: Break the posture to brabo choke variation 2

Often times your opponent will be so aware of the dangers of the brabo choke that he will immediately defend any attempts to pass the collar over his head. Here, Megaton ducks under the collar as a way to counter the attack. Royler then uses another variation of the choke.

1 Royler sets up the brabo choke by passing Megaton's left collar under his armpit and over his head until it is on the right side of Megaton's neck and he can grab it with his right hand.

2 Sensing the imminent choke Megaton ducks his head under Royler's arms until his head emerges on the opposite side, removing the threat. Royler keeps both hands on the lapel – the left hand has the palm facing down and the right one facing up so both thumbs point towards the right.

3 Royler pulls the collar down towards Megaton's chest making sure it stays close to the neck. He uses both hands to feed it as far to the left side as possible. Notice that this time the collar passes under Megaton's neck.

4 Royler turns his torso to the right and reaches over Megaton's head with his right arm and grabs the collar with the right hand. Notice that for the best possible choke Royler grabs the collar as close to the right side and front of the neck as possible so the collar is really tight around Megaton's neck.

5 Royler opens his legs; he keeps the left leg straight and bends the right one to put the right foot on the ground so he can push off it to drive his body away and to the right of Megaton. At the same time Royler pulls the collar with his right hand while using the left forearm to brace and push on the left side of Megaton's neck for the choke. Notice that Megaton's escape direction would be to try to move his head to the left towards Royler's chest but Royler's left forearm prevents him from doing that. Also notice that Royler's legs help him add power to the arm pull of the choke by driving his body away from Megaton.

85. Guard attacks: Sitting guard to choke

Grandmaster Helio likes to say that Gracie Jiu-Jitsu is a game of intelligence and deceit. Since Royler is a great study of his dad's instruction he likes to feign and create traps for his opponents to fall into. This is one of the sneakiest chokes in Gracie Jiu-Jitsu. Royler sets up the choke and actually baits Megaton into passing his guard. When Megaton passes he falls into the trap and is choked.

1 Megaton is attempting to pass Royler's guard His right hand holds one of Royler's pant legs and the left hand grabs the back of the gi near the right shoulder. Royler is sitting up with his feet between Megaton's legs and the right hand on the Megaton's left collar. The left hand is planted back to help move his body in the sitting guard and to protect the pass on the left side.

1 DETAIL: The proper grip is very important for this choke: Royler's right hand grips Megaton's collar with the fingers in and the thumb out and the blade of the forearm touching the side of the neck.

3 Royler tightens the choke as he would a regular cross collar choke. He loops the left leg over Megaton's head and presses down on it with the calf to add pressure to the choke.

2 Megaton starts to pass to Royler's right side. He grabs Royler's right pant leg with his right hand and pulls it out to his right while at the same time he pulls his left hand to the left, forcing Royler to spin in a counterclockwise direction for the pass. As Megaton reaches side-control on Royler's right side, Royler grabs Megaton's right side of the collar with his left hand (thumb in and fingers out with the top blade of the forearm pressing against the side of the neck). The choke is now set!

2 DETAIL: This front view shows Royler's hand and forearm position. Both thumbs point to the right so that the top of the left forearm and the bottom of the right forearm press against the sides of Megaton's neck.

86. Guard attack: Sitting guard to loop choke

The loop choke is a very devious and highly effective submission. It can be applied from a variety of positions but it is especially effective from the sitting-up guard, as Royler shows here. One key to the loop choke is to hold the collar lightly, without much tension on the hand; otherwise you will tip your opponent to your real intentions. The second key to the loop choke is for your opponent's head to dip down, either because you pull it down with your hand or simply because he makes a mistake. You hold the grip and wait for your opponent to make a move that distracts his attention from your collar grip.

1 Royler is in the sitting-up guard position with his feet hooked inside Megaton's thighs. His right hand grabs the right collar and the left hand is braced back to help him move his hips. Megaton grabs Royler's gi pants with his hands and pushes them down to pin the legs in his attempt to pass the guard.

2 Royler notices that Megaton is looking down with his head slightly down as well, and sees the opening for the attack. Royler sits up, pulls Megaton's head down with the left hand, lifts his right elbow up and loops the right arm around Megaton's neck and head.

2 DETAIL: Notice that Royler pushes Megaton's head down and to the right so it goes inside his arm.

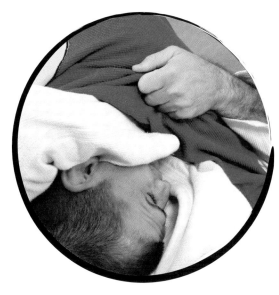

3 **DETAIL:** Notice Royler's left hand grip on Megaton's shoulder keeps him from turning away from the right hand that pulls the collar for the loop choke.

3 Having completely and tightly encircled Megaton's head with his right arm, Royler leans to his left and slides the left hand in front of Megaton's chest and under the left arm. Royler spins his body under Megaton while still pulling on the collar, tightening the noose around the neck. When he is completely under Megaton's chest, Royler is at 180° with Megaton. His right hand applies the choke by pulling the collar tightly. Royler's left hand grabs Megaton's left shoulder and pulls it down to prevent him from rolling over to his right to release the choking pressure.

3 **REVERSE DETAIL** of Royler's twisting motion. Royler dips his head under Megaton's torso and leads with the left arm, driving it in front of the chest and under Megaton's left arm so he can grab the shoulder.

87. Guard attack: Wrist-lock

The wrist-lock is a great way to quickly finish any fight. Because the wrist is a smaller joint than an elbow or a knee, the pressure of the submission is a lot more intense and the opponent has less powerful muscles to use to resist the attack. Because of that the wrist-lock is a favorite of smaller fighter to use against bigger and stronger opponents. In this case Royler surprises Megaton with a clever wrist-lock applied from a break in the posture.

1 Megaton is in Royler's closed guard. His right hand firmly holds Royler's collars at the center of his chest and the right arm prevents Royler from sitting up. Megaton's left hand controls and pulls up Royler's right sleeve as he prepares to stand up to pass the guard.

2 As soon as Megaton makes the slightest movement with his hips to rise and stand up Royler counters to break his posture. Royler coils his legs towards his head, forcing Megaton's torso to fall forward. At the same time Royler uses his right arm to pull Megaton's left arm up and over his head. Megaton ends up with his chest on Royler's chest and the left arm stretched up with the wrist touching the mat above Royler's head.

3 Royler slides the left arm over Megaton's left wrist and locks his left hand onto his own right wrist to secure the figure-4 around Megaton's left forearm and hand. Royler moves his right hand so it holds the top of Megaton's left hand.

4 Royler applies the wrist-lock by bringing his elbows down towards the mat while using the right hand to push Megaton's left hand down and apply pressure to the wrist for the submission.

4 DETAIL: Check out how Royler's right hand pulls Megaton's left hand down at the wrist. The figure-4 lock is positioned so that the blade of Royler's left forearm presses up on the wrist, giving Royler a pivot point to force Megaton's wrist over.

88. Guard attack: Omoplata (shoulder-lock)

The omoplata is one of the staple submissions from the closed guard. When used in conjunction with the triangle and the arm-lock, the omoplata will give you a third solid connected attack from the closed guard, making it very difficult for your opponent to defend your sequence of attacks. Royler here demonstrates the basic omoplata and then proceeds to explore a series of attacks that occur depending on the opponent's counters.

1 Megaton is in Royler's closed guard and has his hands on the ground. Royler grabs Megaton's wrists with his hands. Note: it is not necessary for your opponent's hands to be on the ground for you to use this technique. They may be on your chest or not braced on anything during a transition. The control and the application of the technique will still be the same.

2 Royler opens his guard, unlocking his feet and placing them on the ground. Royler pushes off the right foot to escape the hips to the right while turning his body to the left. Royler's right hand and hips drive Megaton's left arm out to the left, opening it up. Royler drives the left knee in front of Megaton's right arm as if he were going for a triangle.

3 Instead Royler continues pivoting his head towards his right and loops the right leg around Megaton's left arm. Notice that Royler makes sure to keep control of Megaton's left wrist with his right hand otherwise Megaton will pull the arm out to escape Royler's grasp.

4 Royler pushes off his hands to continue to pivot his body to the right until he is at 90° with Megaton's body. He sits up while tucking the right foot in and under his hips.

5 Royler continues to sit forward. His right leg and hips force Megaton's left arm to pivot around the shoulder for the omoplata or shoulder-lock. Royler grabs Megaton's right hip with his right hand to prevent him from rolling forward over his head to escape the pressure.

89. Guard attacks: Omoplata to shoulder-lock variation

Often, when you attempt to apply the omoplata your opponent resists your turning the arm by holding his own belt and lifting you back. In that case Royler has a clever option demonstrated here as he applies the shoulder-lock with a new twist. Notice how Royler makes clever use of his hands to move his body from one side to the other by pivoting on his buttocks.

1 Megaton is inside Royler's closed guard. His hands are on the ground. Royler is able to control Megaton's wrist with his hand. Note: Royler could still use this variation if one of Megaton's hand were loose.

2 Royler wants to attack the left arm with an omoplata. He pushes Megaton's left wrist back to force the arm against his right thigh. He then opens the legs, plants his feet on the mat and pushes off them to escape his hips back and to the right while turning his body to the left. Royler pushes off the left foot to help circle his torso towards his right and loops the right leg around Megaton's left arm. It is very important for Royler to maintain control over Megaton's left wrist with his right hand.

2 (REVERSE VIEW) Notice how Royler grabs Megaton's left wrist with his right hand and pushes it back, forcing the arm to pivot around his thigh.

3 Royler continues to turn to his right, using his hands to help move his body in that direction, until he is almost parallel to Megaton's body. Royler locks the left leg over the right foot to secure the figure-4 hold around Megaton's left arm. Sensing the omo-plata attack on his left arm, Megaton holds his own belt with his left hand and starts to lift his head and torso, preventing Royler from sitting forward and applying pressure to the shoulder. Megaton wants to raise his torso and force Royler to put his back on the mat.

4 Royler pushes off his hands and turns his body back to the left until he is perpendicular to Megaton's body and can extend the left leg and hook the foot under Megaton's right arm.

5 Having locked the foot under Megaton's armpit Royler continues to push off his hands. This time he wants his hips to move back so he can sit up and extend his legs which will push Megaton's shoulder down and force him to go flat on the mat. Royler reaches with both hands and grabs the right side of Megaton's ribcage to help pull himself forward and turning Megaton's torso in a clockwise direction. This forces Megaton's shoulder even more for the submission. Notice that the pressure is applied by the combination of Royler's legs pushing down on Megaton's left arm near the shoulder while the hips push the elbow and forearm up to force the shoulder joint.

90. Guard attacks: Omoplata to wrist-lock

Grandmaster Helio believes in always looking for the path of least resistance. His son Royler is no different. He is always on the lookout for options even when he appears on the verge of securing a finishing hold. Many times as your opponent struggles to defend and escape a submission you may find opportunities to use other submissions, as Royler does here. In this case, he goes for the wrist-lock from the omoplata.

1 Royler attacks Megaton's left arm and shoulder with an omoplata.

2 As he nears the finish Royler embraces Megaton's back with his right arm. At this point, during Megaton's struggle to escape, he holds his own belt with the left hand. Royler grabs Megaton's left elbow with his left hand and secures it in place as he prepares to switch to the wrist-lock.

3 Royler lets go of the embrace and moves his torso away from Megaton. The pressure of Royler's torso moving out forces Megaton's left hand to let go of the belt. Because Megaton's left hand is not holding onto anything and is exposed, it can be attacked.

4 Royler uses his right hand to grab Megaton's left hand and pushes it down towards the mat for the wrist-lock.

4 DETAIL: When applying the wrist-lock you must always secure the opponent's elbow on the same arm of the lock otherwise he will constantly move the forearm away from the pressure. In this case Royler's left hand still controls Megaton's left elbow to secure it in place.

91. Guard attack: Omoplata to toe-hold

Another great option from the omoplata when the opponent struggles to defend is to go for the toe-hold. In this case Megaton has a strong hold on his belt so Royler opts for the toe-hold.

1 Royler attacks Megaton's left arm with an omoplata. Megaton holds onto his belt with his left hand to counter it.

2 Rather than fight to break the grip, this time Royler goes for the toe-hold. He turns his shoulders to his left and grabs under Megaton's left foot with the right hand.

3 Royler lifts Megaton's foot with his right hand and wraps the left arm around the inside of the leg in front of the shin until he can grab his own right wrist with his left hand. Royler now has secured the figure-4 lock around Megaton's left foot.

4 Royler slides the figure-4 as close to the ankle as possible. He closes his elbows tight and applies the toe-hold by pulling the foot in a counter-clockwise direction with his right hand and leveraging it around his own left wrist.

4 DETAIL: Check out Royler's grip on Megaton's foot: the right hand holds the outside edge of the foot near the toes. Royler pushes them down by using the left hand grip on the right hand as a pivot to add pressure to the push. Royler's left forearm blocks Megaton's ankle from moving and gives Royler another fulcrum point for turning the foot around the ankle for the toe-hold submission.

92. Guard attack: Omoplata to crucifix

This time when Royler attacks Megaton with the omoplata, Megaton is able to quickly defend and advance on his counter by holding the belt and raising his torso, which forces Royler back to the mat. Royler uses Megaton's reaction to his own benefit and quickly changes to the crucifix.

1 Royler attacks Megaton's left arm with the omoplata. Megaton reacts quickly and defends by grabbing his own belt with his left hand.

2 When Royler reaches and embraces Megaton's back with the right arm, Megaton quickly steps out with his right leg and pushes off it to raise his torso up and force Royler to fall back to the mat. Notice that Royler's right hand grabs the right side of Megaton's gi near the armpit.

3 Royler turns to his right and uses his right hand to pull Megaton's gi. He slides the hand under Megaton's right armpit.

 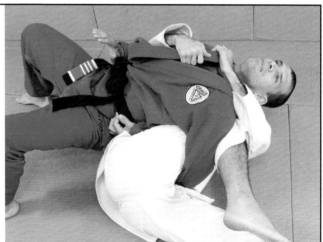

4 Royler grabs Megaton's right collar with his right hand to open it and pull it to the left so he can grab it with his left hand.

5 Royler pulls Megaton's collar down with the left hand while hooking his right arm on Megaton's right arm.

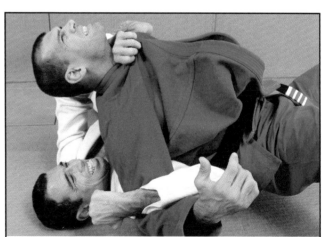

5 (REVERSE VIEW) See how Royler uses the right arm to hook Megaton's right arm so he can't turn to his left and applies the choke while pulling the collar to tighten the choke.

93. Guard attack: Reverse Americana

This is one clever and sneaky submission that will both surprise your opponents and make them worry next time they try to open your guard. Royler takes advantage of Megaton's attempt to break open the legs for the guard pass and goes for the reverse Americana.

1 Megaton is in Royler's closed guard. His left hand controls Royler's collars and the right hand control the hips.

2 Megaton reaches back with the right hand to try to unlock Royler's feet to break open the guard.

3 Royler hooks the right foot on Megaton's arm and kicks it up as he unlocks his feet. With his right leg locking Megaton's right arm in place, Royler plants the left foot on the mat and pushes off it to move his hips to the left and his torso to the right.

4 Royler sits up, grabs Megaton's right arm with his hands and pulls it back towards Megaton's left shoulder.

5 Royler closes his guard as he realigns his body with Megaton's and pulls Megaton's right arm up as if he wanted to touch Megaton's left ear with the right hand for the shoulder-lock, or reverse Americana.

6 (REVERSE VIEW) Notice how Royler has both arms on the left side of Megaton's head. His hands grip Megaton's arm near the wrist.

94. Guard attack: Shoulder lock

It is very common for opponents to reach under your leg and grab your belt in the effort to control your hips and pass your guard. When that occurs if you don't react and counter they will have a great advantage and will probably succeed in passing your guard and reaching your side. Royler demonstrates a quick, effective submission that takes advantage of your opponent's grip.

1 Megaton attempts to pass Royler's guard.

2 He reaches under Royler's right leg with his left arm and grabs Royler's belt while grabbing Royler's left leg with his right hand and pinning it down. If Royler doesn't react Megaton will pass to his right over Royler's left leg.

3 Royler grabs Megaton's left wrist with his right hand.

4 He turns his torso to the right and hooks the right foot on the outside of Megaton's right hip and reaches across his body to grab Megaton's belt with his left hand.

5 Royler stretches the right leg and leans back. His right thigh presses down on Megaton's left arm while his right hand pulls the left wrist up to force the left shoulder.

5 (REVERSE VIEW) Notice how Royler's right foot hooks the outside of Megaton's right hip. This allows Royler the proper angle and control over Megaton's arm and body when he stretches the leg for the submission.

95. Guard attack: Choke variation

Royler likes to choke his opponents just like his dad the Grandmaster. For that reason Royler has used, developed and modified many choke variations. This is one of his favorites as it surprises the opponent because it seems to offer no danger until it is too late and all the opponent can do is submit.

1 Megaton is inside Royler's closed guard.

2 Royler's right hand grabs Megaton's left sleeve above the elbow while his left hand grabs Megaton's right collar with the thumb inside and the fingers on the outside so that the top blade of his forearm aims towards Megaton's neck.

3 Royler opens his legs, plants the left foot on the mat and pushes off it, turning his torso to the right. Royler raises his right leg up towards Megaton's left shoulder. Notice that at this point Royler's left forearm locks under Megaton's throat.

4 Royler loops and locks the left leg over Megaton's head as if he was doing an arm-lock on Megaton except that Royler is choking him with his left hand pulling the collar and forcing the forearm against Megaton's throat while the left leg pushes Megaton's head against the forearm to add pressure to the choke.

96. Guard attack: X-guard takes the back to choke

Royler is never shy of using any technique if it works. In this case Royler uses the X-guard to take Megaton's back and choke him.

1 **Royler has Megaton in his open guard. His right hand controls Megaton's left sleeve and the left hand holds Megaton's right sleeve. Royler's left foot hooks behind Megaton's right knee and his right foot pushes Megaton's left hip back. Megaton has good posture with his head up high and his legs in good base.**

2 **Royler switches to the X-guard. He switches the control over Megaton's left arm to his (Royler's) left hand freeing the right hand so he can underhook the right arm on Megaton's left leg and slide the right knee under Megaton's left thigh.**

3 Royler slides his hips down and ducks his head under Megaton's left knee until it comes out on the other side of the leg. He grabs the back of Megaton's belt with his right hand.

3 (REVERSE VIEW)Check out Royler's leg position: the feet are in an X and control Megaton's right leg. Also notice how Royler holds Megaton's belt with his right hand – the fingers grip over the belt.

4 Royler releases the left hook from the back of Megaton's right leg and pushes off his right foot. He turns his torso to his left until he is centered behind Megaton and has his feet hooked inside Megaton's legs. Royler now grips the belt with both hands.

4 (REVERSE VIEW) Royler's hands grab Megaton's belt while his shins and hooks control Megaton's legs in preparation for the takedown.

5 Royler pulls the belt with his hands and extends his legs. This kicks Megaton's legs out, forcing him to fall backwards. He lands on the mat in front of Royler.

6 Royler loops his legs around Megaton's legs, adding the hooks. He wraps his right arm around Megaton's neck and grabs the left lapel with the hand (thumb in and fingers out).

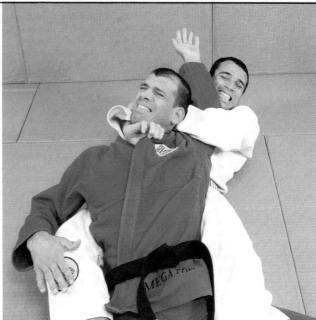

7 Royler slides his left arm under Megaton's left armpit. He bends the arm and turns the hand so the back of it touches the back of Megaton's head. Royler applies the choke by pulling the collar with his right hand while sliding the left arm behind Megaton's head.

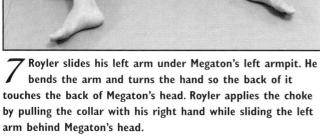

97. Guard attack: Gogoplata

This is a very creative and ingenious submission and it requires a certain amount of hip flexibility. It is quite effective especially against an opponent who is holding on tightly and stalling. It has a similar initial motion as the omoplata but diverts to a choke on the Adam's apple, in Portuguese slang called the "gogo" – hence the name!

1 Megaton is inside Royler's closed guard and has a very tight protective stance with his chest down and his hands under Royler's armpit. Megaton's arms are tight against Royler's side with the elbows almost touching his knees, locking Royler's hips in place.

2 Royler needs to create space and break Megaton's overly defensive posture. He pushes Megaton's forehead with his left hand to force the head and chest away. Royler unlocks his feet and opens his legs. He plants the left heel on the ground and pushes off it to raise his hips slightly.

3 While still pushing Megaton's forehead, Royler curls his right leg back and around Megaton's left arm. Since Megaton is still holding on tightly, Royler needs to help the leg encircle the arm by grabbing his ankle with his right hand.

4 Royler continues to bring his right leg around Megaton's arm by directing his leg with his right hand until the foot slides under Megaton's face and the shin hooks under Megaton's throat. Royler's foot ends up coming out on the right side of Megaton's head. Now Royler's shin blade is pressing against Megaton's Adam's apple.

5 Royler grabs the back of Megaton's head with both hands and pulls it down, forcing the throat against the shin bone for the gogoplata choke.

98. Guard attack: Gogoplata to arm-bar

When applying the gogoplata it is quite common for the opponent to counter it by pulling his head back to prevent you from forcing it down for the choke. When he does that he exposes his arm for this arm-bar.

1 Megaton is inside Royler's closed guard holding on tightly. Royler starts to apply the gogoplata: he pushes Megaton's forehead back, and opens his legs. With the help of his right hand, Royler guides the right leg around Megaton's left arm until the shinbone locks in front of the throat.

2 Sensing the choke coming, Megaton counters by raising his body and head away to prevent Royler from grabbing the back of his head.

3 Royler takes advantage of Megaton's counter. He notices that Megaton's arm is extended and trapped by his right leg with the right armpit locking the wrist. Pushing off his right leg, Royler raises his hips up to force them against Megaton's left elbow and hyperextend it for the arm-bar.

99. Guard attack: Gogoplata to omoplata (shoulder-lock)

An even more experienced fighter when faced with the gogoplata would counter it differently. Not only he would try to move his torso and head away but he would also push Royler's foot down to remove the pressure of the shin against his throat and to prevent Royler from pushing off the leg to raise his hips effectively for the arm-bar. In that case

Royler immediately switches to the omoplata. Notice that Royler always tries to use the simplest follow-up attack to the counter. If Megaton only tries to pull back, he goes for the arm-bar; if Megaton pulls back and pushes the foot down, he has to go for the omoplata.

1 Megaton is inside Royler's closed guard holding on tightly. Royler starts to apply the gogoplata: he pushes Megaton's forehead back, and opens his legs. With the help of his right hand, Royler guides the right leg around Megaton's left arm until the shinbone locks in front of the throat. Royler reaches with his hands and tries to grab Megaton's head.

2 Megaton counters the attack by raising his head and torso while at the same time he pushes Royler's right foot down with his right hand. This releases the pressure of the shinbone on his throat and also compresses Royler's leg back making it impossible to apply the arm-bar. As a result his left arm is protected from the arm-lock.

3 Recognizing the effect of the counter, Royler swings the left leg out and turns to his left side while moving his torso to the right. Royler pushes his right knee down with his right hand and grabs the right shin with his left hand to lock the leg around Megaton's left arm.

4 Royler sits up, swings his legs around and back and embraces Megaton's back with his right arm to prevent him from rolling forward to escape the pressure on the shoulder. Royler continues circling his body around Megaton's left arm. As his legs go back and his hips move forward he torques Megaton's arm around the shoulder for the omoplata.

100. Guard attack: Gogoplata to omoplata to arm-lock (complex)

In Gracie Jiu-Jitsu, at the highest levels opponents will counter one attack after the other until they escape. If you are not ready with a sequence of attacks that anticipates your opponent's counter option and escape avenues, he will more likely succeed in his escape, leaving you frustrated. Royler now shows an advanced sequence of attacks, counters and counter to the counters. This technique is not unique to this position but it serves to illustrate the mind-frame that you should have when attacking an advanced opponent. It also serves to open your mind so you can look for other sequences, similar to this one or not, that can be used in other situations.

1 Megaton is inside Royler's closed guard holding on tightly. Royler starts to apply the gogoplata: he pushes Megaton's forehead back, and opens his legs. With the help of his right hand, Royler guides the right leg around Megaton's left arm until the shinbone locks in front of the throat. Royler reaches with his hands and tries to grab Megaton's head.

2 Megaton counters by raising his torso and pushing Royler's foot down. Royler switches to the omoplata and sits forward with his leg wrapped and locked around Megaton's left arm.

3 Megaton counters the omoplata by rolling forward over his left shoulder to release the torque on his shoulder. Royler pulls his right shin in with the right hand and hooks the foot under his left leg at the knee.

4 Royler leaves his right leg wrapped around Megaton's arm and slides the right elbow over Megaton's trapped left arm.

5 Royler uses both hands to grip Megaton's wrist, keeping it close to his chest as he
leans back until his back touches the mat, and further extends the arm. Royler raises
his hips, pressing them against Megaton's elbow and hyperextending it for the arm-lock.

101. Guard attack: Arm-lock from the open guard

This is a very nice variation of the arm-lock as it takes place from the open guard without getting your hips close to the opponent's body. The cagey opponent knows that generally, in order to be successful with a joint lock, you need to have your hips next to the joint that you are attacking. In this case however Royler cleverly uses the figure-4 to get the leverage for the arm-lock.

1 Megaton is in Royler's open guard. Royler controls Megaton's left arm by using his right hand to hold the wrist and the left hand to grab the elbow.

2 Royler places his left foot on Megaton's right bicep and extends the leg to create distance between himself and Megaton. He extends the left arm at the same time.

3 Royler turns his torso to the right slightly and loops the right leg over Megaton's left arm. He locks the right foot under the left leg at the knee for the figure-4. In order to get the proper leverage for the arm-lock Royler needs to make sure that his right leg loops Megaton's arm above the elbow.

4 Royler pushes off his right leg and raises his hips up to press them against Megaton's left elbow for the arm-lock.

102. Guard attack: Sweep to arm-lock

In this technique Royler uses a very unconventional sweep and then follows up with a submission, the arm-lock. This sweep looks like a failed arm-lock in which the attacker somehow attacks the wrong arm, only to succeed in the sweep instead. Royler's follow-up with the submission will surprise the opponent even more.

1 Megaton is inside Royler's closed guard. Royler grabs Megaton's sleeves with his hands (right hand holds the left sleeve and the left hand holds the right sleeve).

2 Royler switches grips, now using the left hand to grab Megaton's left sleeve while his right hand grabs Megaton's left pant leg at the knee.

3 Royler swings the left leg out and then over Megaton's left arm. Royler ends the initial move kneeling next to Megaton's left side. Notice that Royler remains in control of Megaton's left sleeve with his left hand and also Megaton's left leg with his right hand.

4 Royler continues rolling in a clockwise direction and pulls Megaton over with him. The pressure of Royler's hips against Megaton's arm and Royler's pull on the left leg force Megaton to roll over.

4 DETAIL: Notice Royler's right leg position: the leg bends around Megaton's left arm, the shin presses against the left ribs and the right foot hooks under the left side.

5 Royler hooks his right foot under the left leg with the figure-4 around Megaton's arm and arches his body back while raising the hips against Megaton's left elbow for the arm-lock.